CONCEPTS OF THE ULTIMATE

Concepts of the Ultimate

Edited by Linda J. Tessier

Assistant Professor of Philosophy and Religious Studies
Youngstown State University, Youngstown, Ohio

St. Martin's Press   New York

First published in the United States of America in 1989

Printed in Great Britain

ISBN 0–312–04141–1

Library of Congress Cataloging-in-Publication Data
Concepts of the ulitmate : philosophical perspectives on the nature of
the Divine / edited by Linda J. Tessier.
    p.   cm.
ISBN 0–312–04141–1
1. God—Congresses.   2. Philosophical theology—Congresses.
I. Tessier, Linda J. (Linda Jo)
BT102.A1C67   1989
291.2'11—dc20   89–28754
                                                              CIP

Contents

PART VI

Acknowledgements

The discussions which comprise this volume have emerged out of a gathering of scholars at the annual Claremont Graduate School Philosophy of Religion Conference which took place at Claremont McKenna College in 1986. A number of organizations and individuals helped to make that event an intense and dynamic encounter among scholars interested in considering the ultimate from various religious perspectives. I wish to thank the James A. Blaisdell Programs in World Religions and Cultures at Claremont Graduate School for sponsoring the event along with the Religion Department of Claremont Graduate School and Claremont McKenna College. Certain individuals provided essential assistance in organizing this conference and gathering the scholars who participated, and I especially wish to thank John Hick and Stephen Davis for their help in these areas.

The conference participants have been conscientious and co-operative in providing the comments and responses which follow the initial discussions, and I wish to thank all the participants for their willing attention to deadlines and for their powerful ideas. Professor Hick has also been extremely helpful to me throughout the process of gathering and compiling the presentations, comments and responses through various stages. I also wish to thank the philosophy and religion editors at Macmillan, especially Pauline Snelson and Sophie Lillington, for their patience and most valuable assistance in the process of compiling this book.

Notes on the Contributors

Robert Merrihew Adams is Professor of Philosophy at the University of California, Los Angeles. A collection of his papers in the philosophy of religion has recently been published under the title *The Virtue of Faith and Other Essays in Philosophical Theology*.

John R. Cobb. Jr. is Ingraham Professor of Theology at the School of Theology at Claremont, Avery Professor of Religion at the Claremont Graduate School, Director of the Center for Process Studies, and publisher of the journal *Process Studies*. Among recent books are *Beyond Dialogue* and *Christ in a Pluralistic Age*.

Francis Cook is Emeritus Professor of Religious Studies at the University of California, Riverside, where he taught in the Program in Religious Studies from 1970 to 1988. He has done extensive research in the area of Buddhist studies and is the author of *Hua-yen Buddhism: the Jewel Net of Indra*, *How to Raise an Ox*, and, forthcoming in 1989, *Sounds of Valley Streams*. He is also the author of numerous articles on Hua-yen Buddhism, Zen Buddhism, and articles concerning Buddhist-Christian dialogue. He is currently translating the *Denko-roku*, by the medieval Japanese Zen master, Keizan Jokin.

Margaret Dornish was educated in the study of religion at Yale Divinity School and Claremont Graduate School and studied fine arts at the University of Southern California. She is Associate Professor of Religion at Pomona College and served as the editor of the *Journal* of the Blaisdell Institute. Her work in Buddhism includes extensive research concerning the writings of D. T. Suzuki.

Stephen T. Davis is Professor of Philosophy and Religion at Claremont McKenna College. His books include *Faith, Skepticism, and Evidence: An Essay in Religious Epistemology* and *Logic and the Nature of God*. He is also a contributing editor to *Encountering Evil: Live Options in Theodicy* and *Encountering Jesus: A Debate on Christology* (forthcoming).

David Ray Griffin is a Professor of Philosophy of Religion at the School of Theology at Claremont and Claremont Graduate School, executive director of the Center for Process Studies, and founding president of the Center for a Postmodern World (in Santa Barbara). He is author of *A Process Christology, God, Power, and Evil: A Process Theology, Process Theology* (with John B. Cobb, Jr.), and *God and Religion in the Postmodern World*, and editor of *Physics and the Ultimate Significance of Time, The Reenchantment of Science: Postmodern Proposals*, and *Spirituality and Society: Postmodern Visions*. He is also editor of the SUNY Series in Constructive Postmodern Thought.

John Hick is Danforth Professor and Chair of the Department of Religion at Claremont Graduate School and Director of the James A. Blaisdell Programs in World Religions and Cultures. He has chaired and served on numerous panels and councils involving inter-faith dialogue and has lectured extensively in Great Britain, India and the United States, including the Gifford Lectures in Edinburgh in 1986–87. In addition to appointments at Cornell University, Princeton Theological Seminary, Cambridge University, Gonville and Caius College, Cambridge, and Birmingham University, he has been a visiting professor at various universities in India and Sri Lanka. His numerous publications include *Philosophy of Religion, Evil and the God of Love, God and the Universe of Faiths, Death and Eternal Life, The Myth of God Incarnate, God Has Many Names*, and *Problems of Religious Pluralism*. His most recent book is *An Interpretation of Religion*.

Christopher Ives is Assistant Professor of Religion at the University of Puget Sound. In addition to publication of articles relating to Buddhism and process studies, he has translated a number of Japanese works on Buddhism.

June O'Connor is Associate Professor and Chair of the Program in Religious Studies at the University of California, Riverside. She has authored articles and review essays on theology and religious ethics in a number of journals, including *Religious Studies Review, Cross Currents, Christian Century, Journal of Religion and Culture*, the *Hastings Center Report*, and *Union Seminary Quarterly Review* and has written a book entitled *The Quest for Political and Spiritual Liberation: A Study in the Thought of Sri Aurobindo Ghose*.

Joseph Prabhu is a citizen of India who was educated in economics and politics in Delhi and in philosophy and theology in Germany and Cambridge, England, before getting his PhD in philosophy from Boston University. He is currently an associate professor of philosophy at California State University, Los Angeles, and has taught as visiting professor at United Theological College, Bangalore, India, at the University of California, Santa Barbara, and the Ecumenical Institute of the World Council of Churches. He is editor of the forthcoming work *The Cross-Cultural Understanding of Raimundo Panikkar* and is completing a book on Hegel's political theology for the State University of New York Press.

John K. Roth is the Russell K. Pitzer Professor of Philosophy at Claremont McKenna College. His 16 books include *A Consuming Fire: Encounters with Elie Wiesel and the Holocaust* and *Two Approaches to Auschwitz: the Holocaust and its Legacy* (with Richard L. Rubenstein). He was selected as 1988 Professor of the Year by the Council for Advancement and Support of Education.

Sushanta Sen is a native of West Bengal, India, and was educated at Visva-Bharati University. He has been Professor of Philosophy in the Visva-Bharati University since 1986. He has previously taught as a Lecturer in Indian Religions in the Department of Theology at the University of Birmingham, England, and as a Lecturer at Visva-Bharati. His fields of specialization are Indian Philosophy and Religion, Philosophy of Religion, and Comparative Religion. Publications include *A Study of Universals* (1977) and many journal articles in philosophy and religion.

Karen Torjesen is Assistant Professor of Early Christianity and Women's Studies at Claremont Graduate School and has previously taught at Fuller Theological Seminary, Mary Washington College, and Georg August Universitat, Göttingen, Germany. In addition to numerous journal articles and reviews, she has published a book entitled *Hermeneutical Procedure and Theological Structure in Origen's Exegesis*.

Introduction

Among the various cosmological possibilities which humanity considers, there is one for which many (especially, perhaps, philosophers and theologians) have a particular aversion. This is the suggestion that not only is there no end in sight, but there is in fact no end at all; seeking the most basic truths about the universe, we find the idea of the unlimited series, eternal progression, or infinite regress intolerable. So humanity engages in a search for the ultimate. What is that point beyond which it is impossible to go? What is at the end of the series, beyond which further analysis or division cannot be made? What is final, fundamental, primary? What is the first, the last, the maximum, the best, *ne plus ultra*?

The contributors to this volume approach these questions from various religious perspectives. The papers included here emerge out of a conference which took place early in 1986 at Claremont McKenna College in Claremont, California. This conference, sponsored by the Religion Department and the James A. Blaisdell Programs in World Religions and Cultures of the Claremont Graduate School, brought together various scholars for the purpose of sharing ideas about 'the ultimate' from a religious point of view.

It is not the claim or intention of the participants to exhaust all possible perspectives concerning the ultimate, and no one forum can possibly represent all of the religious traditions which conceptualize these issues. This volume represents one dialogue among many in which these issues are being discussed and perspectives compared. As will be evident from the reading, the contributors are intensely aware of the conflicts which currently exist among religious traditions and the need, from a global perspective, to continue ongoing communication, leading not to a collapse of differences but to a deep recognition and respect for other perspectives.

The papers which make up this volume therefore represent only a few of the many religious perspectives on ultimacy. The first three sections indicate the wide-ranging plurality of perspectives even within a 'single' tradition. From a Christian perspective, there are representatives of classical Christian theism (Stephen Davis), process theology (John Cobb), and Christian feminist theology (June O'Connor). The remainder of the book takes up visions of the ultimate in Hinduism and Buddhism and concludes with John Hick's pluralistic position. Sushanta Sen writes from the perspective of Advaita Vedanta Hinduism, and Christopher Ives discusses the concept of 'Emptiness' in Mahayana Buddhism. John Hick seeks to understand the relationship among differing primary religious concepts of the ultimate, rather than writing from within any one religious tradition. The respondents to these papers also come from differing backgrounds and perspectives.

The format for each section consists of an initial paper and response, followed by questions and comments from other participants. The responses of the original paper writers to these additional critiques are also included. Although all the participants focus their attention upon the issue of ultimacy, the complexity of the subject allows for considerable variety regarding the specific issues that are raised here.

Stephen T. Davis of Claremont McKenna College begins by considering the nature of God and addressing the issue of God's omnipotence. In the context of an ongoing debate with process theology, he argues that 'the notion of an unlimited God is preferable, both theologically and philosophically, to the notion of a limited God'. More specifically, Davis takes the position that God must be all-powerful.

The response to Davis by David Ray Griffin of the School of Theology at Claremont defends the point of view which Davis seeks to refute. Against Davis's position, which Griffin calls 'popular supernaturalistic theism', he defends the 'naturalistic' perspective of process theology. Griffin argues that 'basic causal relations of the world' are eternal features of reality which are neither imposed nor controlled by God. 'God is limited in what God can do by the causal power of the other actualities'.

John B. Cobb, Jr. of Claremont Graduate School and the School of Theology at Claremont articulates process theology's understanding of the nature of reality and then directs that discussion toward a consideration of God's ultimacy. His thinking leads to a discussion of the relationship between God and what Cobb calls, in process terms, 'creativity'. Following Alfred North Whitehead, Cobb asserts that God both acts upon and is acted upon by the world. Creativity, God, and the temporal creatures 'all presuppose one another' in a complex and interrelated reality.

In his response to Cobb, Robert Merrihew Adams of the University of California at Los Angeles questions Cobb's tendency to assign 'the religious contemplation of the being of all things' to Indian traditions, such as Vedanta and Buddhism, as distinct from traditions which focus upon a personal deity. Both Adams and Davis also take issue with Cobb's understanding of material cause in relation to God.

The Christian feminist perspective on the ultimate is represented here by June O'Connor of the University of California, Riverside. She points out that there are many different feminist concepts of God. Women develop religious perspectives out of their own experiences, but these have frequently been trivialized, ignored or erased by traditional Christian structures. O'Connor centres her own discussion on christology, focusing particularly on questions relating to the incarnation of God in Jesus and Jesus's nature as both human and divine.

The response to O'Connor is presented by Karen Torjesen of Claremont Graduate School. While affirming diversity and the importance of experience, both O'Connor and Torjesen assert the responsibility of feminist theology to make some universal claims about human experience and the nature of reality. Torjesen supports many of O'Connor's claims and suggests that 'positing a unique identity between Jesus and God' from a feminist viewpoint requires a new understanding of humanity as it pertains to Jesus and to ourselves.

Sushanta Sen of Visva-Bharati University, West Bengal, then discusses the ultimate from the perspective of Hindu tradition. Sen interprets the Vedic-Upanisadic teachings about the Brahman-Atman identity and suggests an understanding of the relationship between polytheism and monotheism in the Hindu tradition. He argues that behind the great variety of deities in Hinduism there is a fundamental unity. The names and concepts of the gods vary, 'but the Reality underlying these concepts is one and the same'.

Margaret Dornish of Pomona College, Claremont, questions Sen's interpretation of Hindu polytheism, contrasting the Advaita Vedanta position as set forth by Shankara with Ramanuja's 'modified' Vedantic theology. The diversity and multiplicity apparent in the Vedas and in the various Hindu philosophies can be interpreted as a valuable resource rather than being explained away. Dornish's response is followed by a rejoinder in which Sen further interprets Shankara's philosophical system.

Christopher Ives of Claremont McKenna College focuses his approach to the ultimate on the concept of 'emptiness' in Mahayana

Buddhism. This perspective differs significantly from the other points of view which appear in this volume. Utilizing the writings of Nagarjuna, Ives notes that 'emptiness' (sunyata) 'negates the reification of *anything* as an ultimate' (emphasis mine). 'Emptiness' serves as an ultimate primarily in its soteriological aspect. His explication of the meaning of 'emptiness' also leads to a discussion of its ethical implications, highlighting values such as compassion, unselfishness, non-possession, and cosmocentric reverence.

Francis Cook of the University of California, Riverside, extends Ives's views rather than critiquing his position. Presenting what he refers to as a 'chilly and uncompromising' reading of Buddhism, Cook explores liberation as freedom from the bondage caused by fear of non-being and suggests that Buddhist liberation is 'liberation to die'. In other words, 'to abandon the need for security means to radically accept oneself as an impermanent, perishing being'.

This discussion is followed by comments from Stephen Davis and John Hick. Davis suggests that the doctrine of emptiness is inconsistent. John Hick raises a question about the location of the 'chill' in Cook's paper. Enlightenment as set out by Cook is available in principle to all. However, since it must be attained in this life, the fact is that the vast majority of humans do not attain it. Hick asks 'whether the Buddhist picture of our human situation as a whole is really as pessimistic as that'.

In the final section, John Hick of Claremont Graduate School defines 'the ultimate' as 'that putative reality which transcends everything other than itself but is not transcended by anything other than itself'. Considering the ultimate in relation to all the various religious traditions, Hick suggests that each 'stream of religious experience' views 'the Real' through the lens of its own culture and mentality, so that what each tradition describes is not 'the Real *an sich*' but a particular manifestation of the Real to human consciousness. For Hick, the ultimate (or, as he prefers, the Real) is 'the noumenal reality' that functions as the 'ultimate ground' of the 'phenomenological variety of the different traditions'.

Hick's interpretation draws responses from several of the participants. In the formal response to Hick's paper, John Roth of Claremont McKenna College asks the question: 'Can John Hick say what he said?' The basis for this problem, according to Roth, is the fact that Hick posits a noumenal Real which is transcendent to every phenomenal distinction. If this is the case, nothing at all can be said about it. Roth refers to Wittgenstein: 'What we cannot speak about we must pass over in silence'.

Roth's response is followed by comments from Davis, Cobb, Ives and Joseph Prabhu of California State University, Los Angeles. The volume concludes with John Hick's summary reply to all of the 'critical queries and disagreements' which face him.

Although there is great diversity among the views represented in this volume, certain central themes and questions pervade the discussion. One question which all concepts of the ultimate must address is the definition of ultimacy itself. From each perspective, some determination is also made about the *nature* of the ultimate.

Two points can initially be made about ultimacy. First, the concept of the ultimate makes no sense outside of a context of relation. We cannot speak of the ultimate without asking: in relation to what? Secondly, ultimacy is a predicate of something (although, as Ives points out, it might be necessary to distinguish between something and some *thing*). It is a descriptive term, indicating that some entity or entities are most or greatest or final.* Thus, each contributor suggests a position regarding what is ultimate and how it is related, whether the subject in question is process theology's 'democracy of ultimates', Brahman as Hinduism's 'highest, transcendental and impersonal Absolute' or Mahayana Buddhism's rejection of any absolute at all.

One issue which is addressed at several points in this discussion has to do with whether the ultimate must be *one*. The monotheistic traditions claim one ultimate deity, while other traditions either worship many gods or describe the ultimate in terms of an impersonal metaphysical principle. Is there one supreme being or principle, or are there many? Is the one deity or metaphysical principle proclaimed by a particular tradition the *only* one? Is there one ultimate with many names, or do all the deities and metaphysical principles of the great religions exist apart from one another?

Centring his perspective on the teachings of Sankara, Sen sees a fundamental unity among the multiplicity of gods (devas) in Hinduism. 'That which exists is one: sages call It by various names'.

---

* These observations about ultimacy are partially derived from an unpublished paper by Prof. Al Louch entitled 'On the Ultimate, Relatively Speaking' presented at the Claremont Graduate School Philosophy of Religion conference on 'Concepts of the Ultimate' on 31 January 1986.

John Hick concurs with this observation, expanding the perspective beyond Hindu deities to include all the various 'personae' and 'impersonae' of the ultimate in the great religious traditions.

Various respondents to this position question whether all religious traditions can be incorporated in this way. Dornish argues that the various names and forms which express reality must be viewed as having a positive meaning rather than being simply interpreted as false or erroneous. Ives suggests that Zen Buddhism does not clearly fit into Hick's paradigm. In Zen, there is no 'unchanging essence or eternal being' in the universe. Therefore, Ives claims, 'one does not experience an ultimate object or noumenal Real as a phenomenon'.

Assuming that there is some entity that is ultimate, what is its (or her or his) nature? If God is that which is ultimate, must God be unlimited or all-powerful? This question is the centre of the lively ongoing debate illustrated here in the contributions of Stephen Davis and David Griffin. The related issues of human freedom and determinism are raised in Cobb's Chapter 5, 'A Process Concept of God'. Utilizing Biblical, theological and philosophical perspectives, Davis presents various arguments for the claim that God must be unlimited. In order to be worthy of worship, God must be able to accomplish God's purposes, including the ability to prevent evil and to grant petitionary prayer. Griffin argues vehemently against Davis's position, claiming that the concept of an unlimited deity is incoherent. He asks, among other things, whether a God who could have prevented great evil and did not (as in the case of the holocaust) is more worthy of worship than one who cannot always grant petitions?

Another question which emerges in the discussion is the relation of the ultimate to the rest of the cosmos? Is the ultimate immanent in the world or above and beyond it, or both? June O'Connor highlights God's immanence, describing 'a God who affirms the value of embodiment by being embodied, and who fosters the goals of mutuality, interdependent differentiation, equality, and freedom as empowerment'. Emptiness (sunyata) is 'synonomous with dependent co-origination, with the continuous changing system of relationships called "becoming"'. On the other hand, Vedanta Hinduism, as set out by Sen, highlights both the transcendent and immanent aspects of God. In the immanent aspect (Isvara), God remains within the world after creation, pervading and permeating the cosmos. However, God is also beyond the world and in this transcendental aspect (Nirguna Brahman) defies all human measurement, comprehension or description.

This discussion points to other issues relating to the role of the ultimate in creation. Ought the ultimate to be considered as the efficient or material cause of the universe? One thorough discussion of these issues is undertaken here by John Cobb. He challenges the understanding of God as 'the ultimate material cause of all things, that is, the stuff of the world', concluding that 'God may be ultimate in the lines of efficient, final, or formal causes, but not in the line of material causes'. This conclusion leads him to another – that there is an ultimate in addition to God, although this is not to be understood as another God. 'Creativity, God, and the temporal creatures all presuppose one another'.

Implicit in these discussions are other related issues. Several of the participants consider the relationship between the ultimate and the self. These discussions lead in turn to epistemological questions. How can or do we *know* the ultimate? Here revelation has an important role to play, and several writers refer to scriptural authority in developing their perspectives. Others point to the self as a source of knowledge about the ultimate, as in the Hindu concept of the Atman-Brahman identity. June O'Connor makes the important point that cultural images of the ultimate are often inadequate to the experiences of disenfranchised minorities.

Relationality between humanity and the ultimate extends beyond questions of knowledge. How does the power of the ultimate relate to human salvation? What human responses are required in relation to the earth and to one another? What is the meaning of human freedom in relation to the ultimate?

And after all the various perspectives have been set out, what is the meaning of this bewildering plurality of views? Are we faced with a conclusion that one or some of these perspectives are right while others are wrong? Is there a possible complementarity among religious views or a perspective which can adequately encompass all of them without denying their essential validity? In its affirmation of these powerful diversities, this volume reaches no agreed conclusion regarding these questions.

Part I

1

Why God Must Be Unlimited

Stephen T. Davis

Suppose we agree that God exists, that is, that there is a person called God. The natural thing for us to wonder next is: what is God like? what are God's properties? how should we describe God? is God limited or unlimited? These are important questions precisely because among people who believe in God there are various theories about the divine nature. Some of these widely divergent theories are to be found even among Christian theologians.

As a rough taxonomy of degrees of divine limitation (moving from most to least limited), we might suggest the following: (1) the gods of the ancient Greek pantheon. More powerful and wiser than humans, these beings were nevertheless fallible in power, wisdom and goodness. Even Zeus was subservient to fate; (2) the God of process theology, that is, the God of Whitehead, Hartshorne, Cobb, *et al.*, a loving and powerful but nevertheless severely limited God. I shall argue against notions of God like this one; (3) the God of classical Christian theism, that is, the God of Augustine, Aquinas, Calvin, Barth, *et al*. My main aim in this paper is to argue on behalf of this sort of conception of God; (4) the God of Descartes. I shall not discuss this conception of God, that is, a being unlimited even by the canons of logic, holding as I do (along with most people who discuss omnipotence) that it is incoherent.

I take it that there is a broad consensus among most Christians (and surely other theists as well) on certain criteria of divinity. In order to be God a being must be (1) very powerful (far more powerful than human beings); (2) the creator of the heavens and the earth (though there are various notions of what is meant by 'create'); (3) everlasting (this term too is interpreted in various ways); and (4) loving, compassionate, gracious, morally good. Beyond these points, however, Christians seem to differ on the question whether we ought to speak of God as *unlimited*.

I

But what is meant by terms like 'limited' and 'unlimited' when applied to beings? What exactly is an 'unlimited being'? Well, we should not press the term in too literal a direction; doubtless the notion of 'a being without any limitations at all' is incoherent. Even the beings theologians typically speak of as unlimited (for example, the God of classical Christian theism) are limited in some ways – there are, for example, certain things they cannot do. The term 'unlimited being', then, seems mainly a way of distinguishing one sort of conception of God from another, for example, distinguishing the God of classical Christian theism from the God of process theology.

There are at least two ways in which we might try to define the term 'unlimited being'. The first and far more simple way is to say that an unlimited being is one that is not bound by causal constraints. Such a being might still be bound by logical constraints and so will be unable to do things like create a married bachelor or bring it about that the sum of 6 and 5 is 13. But such a being will be quite unrestrained by the causal laws which prevent human beings from doing things like parting the waters of the sea or raising the dead. One difficulty with this way of understanding the term 'unlimited', however, is that only *power* is taken to be relevant; and possibly what makes a being 'unlimited' is more than just omnipotence – perhaps maximal degrees of knowledge, wisdom, goodness and so forth must be included, too.

The notion of 'maximal degree' leads directly to a second way of understanding the notion of an 'unlimited being'. Let us first notice that some properties of beings are relevant to the greatness or likeness to God of those beings and some are not. The property of *being red-headed*, for example, is not (as we might say) a great-making or Godlike-making property because a red-headed being is not (other things being equal) necessarily greater or more Godlike than a non-red-headed being. But other properties clearly are relevant to the greatness or Godlikeness of the beings that have them. The property of *being all-powerful*, for example, is a great-making or Godlike-making property because an all-powerful being *is* (other things being equal) necessarily greater or more Godlike than a being that is not all-powerful. Let us call these sorts of properties, properties that make the beings that have them greater or more Godlike, G-properties.

Let us also notice that some properties admit of degrees or increments and others do not. For example, the property of *being a prime number* admits of no degrees – a being either possesses it or does not. The same would be true of properties like *being pregnant*, *being six feet tall*, *being either a horse or a non-horse*, and so on. But some properties do admit of degrees, for example, *being tall*. Some tall people are taller than other tall people. The same would be true of the property of *being a composite number as much greater than six as possible* – some composite numbers greater than six (for instance, 18) are greater than other composite numbers greater than six (for instance, ten).

Now of the properties that admit of degrees, we notice that some of them possess, so to speak, an intrinsic or conceivable maximum and some do not. For example, the property of *being tall* possesses no intrinsic maximum – no matter how tall we imagine a tall person to be we can always imagine one taller. But some properties do possess an intrinsic maximum – for instance, the property of *having scored well in a golf match*. A score that cannot be bested would be achieved by that golfer who scores 18 in an 18-hole match, that is, who makes a hole-in-one on each hole. Perhaps the property of *being powerful* is also such a property. A being who is omni-powerful or omnipotent at a given time (I would say) is a being who can bring about any state of affairs that it is not logically impossible for that being to bring about at that time. This is a degree of power that cannot be bested.

We are now in a position to state our second way of defining the notion of an unlimited being. An unlimited being, we might say, is (1) a being who possesses all the G-properties that it is possible for a being to possess; (2) a being all of whose G-properties that admit of an intrinsic maximum are possessed to the maximal degree (for example, being omnipotent); and (3) a being all of whose G-properties that admit of no intrinsic maximum are possessed to a degree unsurpassed by any other being that has ever existed or ever will exist (for instance, being more loving than any other actual being).

Now despite the earlier caveat about unlimitedness being broader than omnipotence, the sort of unlimitedness in God which I want to argue for in this chapter is primarily unlimitedness in power, that is, omnipotence. This is the sort of property typically denied God by contemporary defenders of a 'limited God' (though the term 'omnipotent' is sometimes retained). Notice too that the first definition of 'unlimited' discussed above (the one about freedom from causal constraints) directly entails omnipotence; and the second definition (the one that concerns the way a being possesses its G-properties) also clearly entails it. Accordingly, either definition will do for my purposes here.

II

What I want to argue is that the notion of an unlimited God is preferable, both theologically and philosophically, to the notion of a limited God. There are, I think, four ways in which one might argue in favour of the proposition that God is unlimited. (1) One might argue that it has been revealed by God that God is unlimited; (2) one might offer a natural theological argument on behalf of the conclusion that God is unlimited; (3) one might raise philosophical or theological criticisms of 'limited God' notions; or (4) one might offer a pragmatic or practical argument on behalf of the conclusion that God is unlimited. Now it cannot be denied that arguments of each sort have been offered in the history of theology that are feeble and unconvincing. I see promise in each approach, however, and wish to explore possibilities in each category.

(1) First, then, one might argue that it has been revealed by God that God is unlimited. And it surely does seem, in a Christian context, that there is ample scriptural material that would naturally lead those who hold to any fairly sturdy view of biblical authority toward the theory that God is unlimited (at least in power). For example, Job says of God: 'I know that thou canst do all things, and that no purpose of thine can be thwarted' (Job 42:2). And the psalmist says: 'Our God is in the heavens; he does whatever he pleases' (Ps. 115:3). Jeremiah says to God: 'Nothing is too hard for thee' (Jer. 32:17). Jesus says: 'With God all things are possible' (Matt. 19:26). And Paul speaks of 'the immeasurable greatness' of God's power (Eph. 1:19).

But in the current theological context, there are severe difficulties such an argument would face. For one thing, the Bible is not a work of philosophy of religion or even of systematic theology; few and perhaps none of the biblical writers faced the precise question we are here exploring ('Is God limited or unlimited?'). Thus their writings (it might be said) are not particularly helpful in the present debate. For another, the Bible notoriously can be and is interpreted in a great variety of ways. Texts which might be quoted on one side or the other of the debate can always be interpreted in other ways. Finally, at least some of those who would argue on behalf of a limited God do not particularly care *what* the Bible says; accordingly, an appeal to revelation will not impress them. Thus David Griffin says: 'The results of the historical-critical approach to the Bible that has been carried out in the past two centuries make it very difficult to consider it (the Bible) an external guarantee for any particular doctrines'.[1]

III

(2) A second way of pressing for an unlimited God is to offer an argument from natural theology to the effect that an unlimited being exists or that a God who is already known or believed to exist must be unlimited. Richard Swinburne offers such an argument in *The Existence of God*,[2] and so have other philosophers and theologians. Undoubtedly the most famous effort in this direction, however, is Anselm's ontological argument (OA); it is this argument that I propose to discuss.

I choose this argument for two reasons. The first is that Anselm clearly intended it as a proof not only of the existence of God but of God's properties (or at least some of them) as well. In his prayer at the beginning of *Proslogion* II he says: 'And so, Lord, do thou . . . give me . . . to understand that thou art as we believe; and that thou art that which we believe'.[3] And what is it that 'we' believe about God, according to Anselm? It is that God is 'a being than which nothing greater can be conceived' (a term that surely either has no referent at all or else has as its referent an unlimited being). The second reason I choose to discuss this argument is because I consider certain versions of it sound – or at least I do not think they have ever been refuted. Though I suspect few philosophers would agree with this, I think most would now grant (after the last 20 years of work on the OA) that Anselm's argument has at least turned out to be an extraordinarily difficult argument to refute.

Now the OA will constitute a successful proof of the existence of an unlimited being if, and only if, two conditions are satisfied: (1) the notion of 'a being than which nothing greater can be conceived' is a coherent notion whose referent is an unlimited being; and (2) the OA itself is a sound argument. (I recognize that the second condition includes the first – the OA couldn't very well be sound if Anselm's term for God were incoherent – but it will be useful to proceed as if we had two separate conditions here.) Now obviously it is not possible for me in the present chapter (or perhaps elsewhere) to demonstrate the soundness of the OA, though, looking back, I see that I have defended the argument against various criticisms on an alarming number of occasions.[4] All I can say is that I *think* there are sound versions of the OA and that I am ready to defend them against whatever criticisms anyone cares to raise.

What does Anselm mean by the term 'a being than which nothing greater can be conceived'? As is obvious, this is a complex term, one that requires a good bit of explication. One thing to note is that Anselm clearly did not mean the greatest being that can be adequately imagined by you or me. Our conceiving or imagining abilities are limited; perhaps we are quite unable to conceive (in some sense of the term 'conceive') of the being Anselm has in mind. But this need not bother Anselm; what he meant was the greatest being that it is logically possible to conceive of by *any* conceiver. It will not trouble Anselm one bit if there are senses of the term 'conceive' where only 'a being than which nothing greater can be conceived' will be able to conceive of 'a being than which nothing greater can be conceived'.

Since philosophers who discuss the OA often refer to Anselm's 'a being than which nothing greater can be conceived' (let's call it ABTW for short) as the 'greatest conceivable being' (GCB) or the 'greatest possible being' (GPB), we might discuss briefly the appropriateness of this move. There are two (closely related) issues here – first, are the logical properties of the terms ABTW, GCB and GPB the same or at least so very nearly the same as to justify their exchangeability? And second, are the limits of conceivability equal to the limits of possibility?

On the first question, there is one point where the terms ABTW and GCB seem to differ in their implications. The term GCB entails that the being in question *can be conceived* (by some conceiver or other) while the term ABTW does not entail this. But this surely is merely a momentary irritant. Let us assume a premise that seems (to me, at least) quite beyond reproach, despite the fact that it is not an explicit part of Anselm's argument, viz., that *ability to conceive of oneself is a G-property*. That is, if we have two beings, A and B, who are alike in greatness as much as possible except that A is able to conceive of itself and B is not, then A is greater than B. If so, then it follows that for any being that cannot conceive of itself, no matter how great this being is, we can conceive of a greater being, viz., one just like it in every possible way except that it *is* able to conceive of itself. The ABTW, then, *must* be a being that can conceive of itself, and the two terms ABTW and GCB turn out to be equivalent.

The second point is far more thorny and complex. There are many things that might be meant by the word 'conceivable' and several things that might be meant by the word 'possible'. By 'possible' let's just stipulate that we mean 'logically possible' in the sense of broad logical possibility standardly used by most philosophers these days.[5] It is possible for me to run the mile in two minutes flat but not for me to meet a married bachelor or truthfully to say, 'I am Richard Nixon'. But clearly we can, if we want, draw the limits of conceivability wider than the limits of possibility (I can *conceive*, in some sense of that term, of married bachelors) or equal to them (married bachelors, in this sense of the term, are *inconceivable*).

By the term 'conceivable', we might mean something like 'logically possible'; something like 'mentally picturable'; something like 'definable'; or something like 'nameable'. Anselm himself seems to use the term in both of the first two ways. He claims in *Proslogion* IV that in one sense of the word 'conceivable' (what he calls 'conceiving of the word') at least one logical impossibility can be conceived (the fool can conceive of God's non-existence). But as long as philosophers make clear their usage and stick to it consistently, I see no serious difficulty in their simply stipulating that for them conceivability equals possibility. (Perhaps this is precisely what Anselm himself does for the other use of the term 'conceive' – 'conceiving of the thing' – he mentions in *Proslogion* IV. This is the sense in which he supposes that the non-existence of God is inconceivable.) I propose in this chapter to make this very move; I will stipulate that conceivability equals possibility; and so I will feel no compunction in using the term GCB in my discussion of the OA.

The final difficulty I will discuss in coming to grasp the meaning of Anselm's term 'a being than which nothing greater can be conceived' is the word 'greater'. Sadly, this is one of the gaps in Anselm's argument; Anselm nowhere tells us exactly what he means by 'greater' or what it is that constitutes 'greatness' for a being. But we

can, as it were, try to work backwards and figure out what he must
have meant or at least what his argument requires. That is, we can
ask what notions of 'greatness' might make the OA succeed. There
is some textual evidence that Anselm wants us to interpret 'greatness' in terms of 'goodness',[6] but I prefer to follow another path. If
we read greatness as, say, *red-headedness* or *running speed* or *largeness*
the OA will clearly not succeed. (There logically can be no 'red-
headedest conceivable being', 'fastest running conceivable being',
or 'largest conceivable being'.) But if we read greatness as *power,
ability, freedom of action* (where the GCB is then omnipotent), the OA
just might succeed. (Perhaps other notions of greatness will also
make the OA succeed.) I make no exegetical claim that this notion of
'greatness' is Anselm's intended notion, although it is clearly in the
spirit of the concept of God he works with in the *Proslogion* and the
Monologion. I claim merely that my criterion is intelligible and has a
chance of allowing the OA to succeed.

Now if all this gives us a reasonably helpful handle on the
meaning of Anselm's term 'a being than which nothing greater can
be conceived', we must proceed to the next question, viz., is the
term coherent? That is, does the notion of a GCB so much as make
sense? The notion will make sense, I think, on two conditions.[7]
First, it must be the case that beings are comparable or commensurable with respect to greatness; and second, it must be the case that
greatness admits of a maximal case. I believe that both conditions
are satisfied. Though much of the groundwork has been done
above, let me explain further.

Clearly, there are notions of greatness on which beings are not
readily comparable. Suppose we say that one being is greater than
another if it is *more of a prime number* than the other. But how can one
being (say, the number three) be *more of a prime number* than another
being (say, the number seven)? An OA based on *this* notion of
greatness cannot even get going. But if we define greatness as
above, that is, as *power, ability, freedom of action*, comparisons clearly
can be made, even among beings of widely different kinds. In some
cases it will be difficult to decide (Is a possum more powerful than a
raccoon?), and in nearly all cases it will be difficult to be mathe-
matically precise (Exactly how much more powerful is a typewriter
than a nail?). Nevertheless, we do frequently compare different
items as to their power, ability to act, freedom, and so forth. Geese
are more powerful than stones; humans are more powerful than
cocker spaniels; President Bush is more powerful than Mayor Koch.

Furthermore, as Tom Morris[8] has recently pointed out, Anselm's argument can go through even if for some reason it is false that all beings are commensurable, that is, even if there are some beings that cannot sensibly be compared with each other in greatness. All Anselm strictly needs is that all beings be comparable in greatness with God. So even if there are two beings, X and Y, that are not comparable with each other in greatness (that is, it makes no sense to ask which of them is greater), the OA can still succeed just as long as it is still true that both X and Y are less great than the GCB.

Is greatness a property that admits of a maximal degree? Surely not on some notions of greatness. But on the notion of greatness I have been using, I believe it does. There logically can be no more powerful being than a being who is omnipotent, as defined above. It looks, then, as if both conditions for the coherence of the concept of the GCB are satisfied. Beings *are* comparable with respect to greatness (as defined), and greatness (as defined) *does* admit of a maximal case. Thus if the term GCB refers to an unlimited being, and if there are sound versions of the OA (naturally, the latter is a very big if), we have found in the OA a piece of natural theology that successfully argues for the existence of an unlimited being.

IV

Now since I am defending the OA in this chapter, I owe it to the reader to present what I consider a sound version of that argument. So let me now briefly do that. It is important to note at the outset that the OA is what we might call an '*a priori* existential' argument. That is, it is an argument that tries to prove the existence of something (viz., the GCB), and it tries to do so primarily by *a priori* means, that is, by examining concepts or ideas or definitions. (This is as opposed to a more common '*a posteriori* existential' argument, one which argues for the existence of something on the basis of probabalistic appeals to experience.) The OA I will present here is a version of the so-called 'first form' of Anselm's argument, the one that is to be found in *Proslogion* II; that is, the argument that follows is my attempt to state, as cogently and clearly as I can, the argument that Anselm presents there.

The argument begins with:

(1) *Things can exist in only two ways – in the mind and in reality.*

A thing exists 'in the mind' if somebody imagines, defines or conceives of it. A thing exists 'in reality' if it is real independently of anyone's ideas or concepts of it. Thus there are four (what we might call) 'modes of existence' – a thing might exist both in the mind and in reality (for example, Ronald Reagan); it might exist in the mind but not in reality (for instance, Stephen Davis's ninth daughter); it might exist in reality but not in the mind (for instance, some undiscovered but existing chemical element); or it might exist in neither way (for example, nuclear weapons in the year AD 1550).

The argument continues with:

(2) *The GCB can possibly exist in reality, that is, is not an impossible thing*.

All premise (2) means is that since we can find no contradiction or other sort of incoherence in the term 'greatest conceivable being', it looks as if this being can possibly exist. It either exists in reality or else (like unicorns and my ninth daughter) contingently fails to exist. Unlike married bachelors and square circles (whose definitions *are* contradictory), logic does not require the non-existence of the GCB. The next premise is:

(3) *The GCB exists in the mind*.

This simply means that someone (Anselm, you the reader, or whoever) has conceived of the GCB. Of course, Anselm is not suggesting that anyone conceives of God in the sense of understanding all about God – as a Christian theologian, he knows no human can do that. He simply suggests that someone has conceived of God in the sense of understanding Anselm's term for God, 'greatest conceivable being'.

The next premise might be called Anselm's hidden premise, because he nowhere states it in the *Proslogion*. It is clear, however, that his argument needs some such step as:

(4) *Whatever exists only in the mind and might possibly exist in reality might possibly be greater than it is*.

The intuitive idea here is that things are greater if they exist both in the mind and in reality than they are if they exist just in the mind. Anselm is not comparing different sorts of things – he is not saying, for example, that a given clod of dirt, since it exists in both ways, is greater (in the sense defined earlier) than Paul Bunyan, who exists only in the mind. He is comparing the same thing in different modes of being – he is saying, for example, that the clod of dirt is greater than it would be if it existed only in the mind, and that Paul Bunyan would have been greater than he in fact is had the legendary woodsman existed in reality as well as in the mind. In terms of our earlier definition of 'greater', Anselm should accordingly be taken as suggesting that things that exist both in the mind and in reality are more powerful, freer, more able to do things than they would be if they existed merely in the mind.

Premises (1) through (4) constitute the basic assumptions of the OA. Like any deductive argument, the soundness of the OA depends on the truth of its assumptions. If any of them is false, the argument is unsound. Next Anselm suggests a premise that he wants to reduce to absurdity:

(5) *The GCB exists only in the mind*.

Anselm thus asks us in effect to assume that the GCB does not exist. He does this because he thinks this assumption, together with the earlier premises of the OA, will lead to a contradiction. *Reductio ad absurdum* is a well-recognized logical device which allows us to negate any premise that is responsible for producing a contradiction or other absurdity. Thus Anselm is trying to prove that the GCB exists by showing that premise (5) (together with (1) through (4)) entails a contradiction.

The next three premises constitute the logical outworking of the assumptions of the OA. Here Anselm shows that premise (5) is unacceptable and should be negated. First, he suggests that if premises (5), (2) and (4) are true, then the premise

(6) *The GCB might be greater than it is*

must be true as well. Now because there might be confusion at this point, let me explain in a bit more detail. Clearly we are able to use and understand the term 'GCB'; the question is what ontological status to assign to the term – or rather to that to which it refers (if it refers to anything). Is the GCB a *mere concept* (like 'Stephen Davis's ninth daughter') or rather an *existing thing* (like 'Stephen Davis's second son')? Note that existing things are *greater* (in the sense of 'greater' defined above) than the concepts of those things. That is, existing things are more powerful, freer, more able to do things than the mere concepts of those things. Mere concepts presumably have some abilities – they can sometimes cause us to think or act, for example – but not nearly so many as existing things. What premise (6) claims, then, is as follows: the ontological status that the GCB has (given premise (5)) is such that (given premise (2)) the GCB might be an existing thing rather than a mere concept; and if it were an existing thing, then (given premise (4)) it would be greater than it is.

As a mere concept, the GCB is not particularly great; as an existing thing it would be greater.

But it can be pointed out that this is to open the OA to an objection. What is needed to make the OA work, it will be said, is that something like the following proposition be coherent:

(6a) *The mere concept of the GCB might be an existing thing*.

But it will then be charged that (6a) is incoherent – a concept cannot literally *be* an existing thing. What does make sense (it will be said) is:

(6b) *The mere concept of the GCB might be an instantiated concept*

(that is, a concept that names or refers to or corresponds to an existing thing), which does not help the OA at all. For Anselm apparently makes no claims about the greatness of concepts (for instance, about instantiated concepts being greater than uninstantiated concepts); rather, he claims that existing things are greater than the mere concepts of those things. If (6a) is incoherent (so the objection concludes), then (6) cannot be coherently stated, and the OA fails.

But in answer to this objection we need only ask what is meant or referred to by the term 'GCB'. If there exists in reality no GCB, then the term 'GCB' of course refers to or denotes a mere concept (the GCB exists, as Anselm would have it, only 'in the mind'). And if the GCB exists (as he would say) 'in reality', then of course the term 'GCB' refers to or denotes an existing thing. Accordingly, Anselm need push no arguments and need have no opinion about whether instantiated concepts are greater than uninstantiated ones. He *does* need to argue, however, that existing things are greater than the concepts of them. His point, then, is that if the GCB *is* a mere concept it is still true that the (non-existent) thing described by that concept might exist (just as Stephen Davis's ninth daughter might possibly exist); and that if it did exist, it would be greater than it (the mere concept) in fact is. It is true that premise (6a) sounds odd – perhaps a concept cannot literally *be* an existing thing, but the point is that the thing the concept describes or refers to might be an existing thing.

But of course this is to invite the following query: what exactly is this 'thing' that the concept describes or refers to? In reply, let's look at what we've thus far said about this 'thing'. We've said it is non-existent; we've said it possesses properties (a non-existent GCB, for example, still has the property of *being a being*); and we've said it can be referred to. But can we refer to non-existent, property-bearing things? Of course we can. The following sentences are not only coherent but true: 'Paul Bunyan is a woodsman', 'Davis's ninth daughter is a daughter'. The 'thing' the concept describes or refers to, then, is simply what we might call a 'possibly existing thing' (dare we call it a PET, for short?). A possibly existing thing is simply a set of compossible properties that might or might not be real (or exist in reality, as Anselm would say). I am a PET, and so is Ronald Reagan; Paul Bunyan is a PET, and so is my ninth daughter. There certainly can be mere concepts of PETS, but a PET is not just and without remainder a mere concept, for surely there are PETS of which no conceiver has ever had any concept. Thus a non-existent GCB can best be thought of as a set of compossible properties that constitute a PET. And premise (6) is to be taken as saying that the GCB, a non-existent PET, might be an existing PET; and that if it were an existing PET, it would be greater than it in fact is.

Having returned to premise (6), let us notice that it is at least implicitly contradictory; what it says is that 'the greatest conceivable being might be greater than it is'. Another way of expressing this implicit contradiction, and one that is directly entailed by premise (6), is:

(7) *The GCB is a being than which a greater is conceivable.*

Now since (7) is an explicit contradiction, then by *reductio ad absurdum* we are allowed to search for whatever premise above it in the argument is responsible for producing the contradiction. Clearly (5) is the culprit; if so, then *reductio ad absurdum* allows us to negate it.

One way of negating a statement is simply to place the phrase 'it is false that' in front of it. Thus we can negate (5), the offending premise, by means of:

(8) *It is false that the GCB exists only in the mind.*

We are now almost finished. We know by premise (1) that things can exist in only two ways, in the mind and in reality; we know by premise (3) that the GCB exists (at least) in the mind; and we know by premise (8) that it is false that the GCB exists only in the mind. Thus it follows that:

(9) *The GCB exists both in the mind and in reality,*

which was what we were trying to prove.[9]

V

(3) A third way of arguing in favour of an unlimited God is to point out difficulties in conceptions of limited Gods. This is a route I am

much inclined to follow, for there is a nagging problem faced by limited God theologians that in my view has never been solved.[10] The difficulty appears most clearly in discussions of the problem of evil. On the one hand, the theodicy project of limited God theologians will only succeed if God is sufficiently impotent to make God (in Griffin's words) 'not indictable' for the evil that exists; God must be weak enough to be incapable of unilaterally preventing evil from existing. But on the other hand the question then emerges whether a being this impotent is God or is worthy of our worship. Such a being can surely be *pitied* – God is working very hard to bring about a better world but doesn't seem to be getting anywhere. Evil runs rampant.

Power, of course, is not the only criterion for worthiness of worship – an omnipotent moral monster (like Descartes' 'Evil Genius') would not merit our worship. But power surely is *one* of the relevant criteria – we would not be much inclined to worship a morally perfect being who was about as powerful as a typical human being, either. As a matter of horseback sociology, it seems to me that limited Gods work best and appeal most in times of high-flying optimism. The idea is that 'we'll all work together with God to make a better world'. But in times of pessimism and even despair like ours, where the vast majority of us feel able to do precisely nothing to prevent the world's destruction, limited views of God seem to me to produce only a kind of melancholy desperation.

Now those who defend limited views of God will doubtless reply to this criticism. The first move they typically make is to ridicule the idea of omnipotence or the worship of power *per se*.[11] But of course, as just noted, the worship of power *per se* is not what I am recommending. They also stress that their God is worthy of worship in virtue of both God's moral goodness and the persuasive power God in fact has (power, for example, to lure the universe towards greater value). But it is still true that their God is quite unable to do things like part the waters of the sea or bodily raise the dead. Finally, they argue that the sort of persuasive power their God has is the highest degree of power any being can possibly have. But this argument turns out to depend on a questionable assumption, viz., that all power must be shared, that all actual beings have power of their own over against God. But why is it logically impossible for God to have all the power?

The notion that God possesses all the power and voluntarily shares it with the creatures seems to me perfectly conceivable. It may or may not be *true* (I believe it is), but it is surely *possibly true*. But

Griffin argues[12] that in the world as it actually is, human creatures *do* have power of their own over against God (and this is certainly true); why not (he asks) simply assume that this truth is a *necessary* truth? But is this a strong argument? I think not. Is it helpful to take truths that we know at least to be contingently true and suppose that they are also necessarily true? It is *true* that kangaroos exist; does it then make sense to imagine that they *necessarily* exist? It is *true* that grass is green; does it then make sense to imagine that grass is *necessarily* green? In fact, even the picture of power entailed by a rigid and all-encompassing predestinarianism seems a possible picture. Perhaps, contrary to appearances, God has *all* the power and shares none of it; perhaps every action apparently taken or decision apparently made by some x is really taken or made by God. I do not myself hold that this picture is a *true* picture, but it is surely a *possible* picture. And if so, the traditional concept of omnipotence is coherent, and a limited God still seems unworthy of worship.

VI

(4) A final way of arguing on behalf of an unlimited God typically strikes some of the same notes. It is to argue on pragmatic grounds that religion, or at least Christian religion, needs an unlimited God. To be 'religiously adequate', it could be said, God must be unlimited as opposed to limited. Some of the arguments that have been presented along these lines are not particularly convincing (see Findlay's argument to the effect that God must be a necessary being);[13] and perhaps all of them are of limited value because of the obvious fact that people differ in their notions of 'religious adequacy'. Nevertheless, I will suggest one such pragmatic argument here; we can call it the 'petitionary prayer argument'.

To be religiously adequate, I claim, God must be the sort of being to whom it makes sense to address petitions. Surely that will be granted by all Christians. And I will argue further that God is not God and is not religiously adequate unless God is in a position to hear and grant our petitions. That, too, will perhaps be allowed. But what sorts of petitions? Here is where I will say something which limited God theologians will not allow. I want to suggest that no God is worthy of worship and is religiously adequate unless granting the following sorts of petitions is within God's power:

a. petitions for healing from disease
    (not just psychosomatic disease)
b. petitions for forgiveness from sin
    (even heinous sin)
c. petitions for deliverance from death
    (that is, for eternal life)
d. petitions for prevention of the world's
    destruction.

Naturally, I do not say a religiously adequate God is under obligation to *grant* all such petitions; my point is just that such a God must be *able* to do so. Otherwise, God is not God, or at least is not worthy of the worship, love and obedience Christians believe we owe God. Now, as noted above, this sort of argument is subject to severe limitations. One such limitation is that it will convince few of those who defend conceptions of limited Gods. Such people can always deny that these sorts of petitionary prayers make sense anyway. Asking God to heal your father of his apparently terminal cancer makes about as much sense as asking God in 1989 to bring it about that atomic weapons were never invented – so it could be said. Nevertheless, I find the petitionary prayer argument convincing and am prepared to defend it. It is, I think, a very strong argument indeed against conceptions of limited Gods – they are just not able to do all the things asked for.

Must God be *unlimited* (as defined earlier) in order to be able to grant such requests? Surely unlimited in the first sense (free from the causal constraints that prevent human beings from doing the things requested); but possibly not in the second sense (having to do with the way God possesses God's G-properties). Nevertheless, I will take it that any God who can grant the above petitions is 'unlimited' (in its power, in any case) in the religiously relevant sense of that term. Such a God (as long as this being also possesses the other properties mentioned in the third paragraph of this chapter) will be acceptable to me. Now my own view, of course, is that God is unlimited in both senses. My present point is that a religiously adequate God *need* only be unlimited in the first sense.

A much larger point – one that is not limited to petitionary prayer – is involved here. To be religiously adequate, it would surely seem that God must be able to accomplish God's purposes. But if God is limited in power, then quite possibly there are not only prayers God will not be able to answer but creatures God will not be able to control and divine aims God will not be able to achieve. If God is limited in power, then neither God nor we who worship God know whether God's purposes, aims and hopes for the world will be fulfilled. To put it bluntly: there is no good news in the news that God is trying very hard and just might succeed. Of course this argument (like the petitionary prayer argument) does not show that it is logically impossible for a limited God to exist. What it shows, I claim, is that limited Gods are religiously inadequate and provide no good news for those who worship them.

VII

We have now discussed four ways in which it might be argued that God ought to be thought of as unlimited rather than limited. It has emerged that there are difficulties with each. (1) The argument that God's unlimited nature has been revealed by God faces the problem that the Bible can be variously interpreted and that at least some of those who believe in a limited God do not particularly care what the Bible says. (2) The ontological argument may turn out to be unsound, as surely is the opinion of most philosophers. (3) The objections I raised against the notion of a limited God may be subject to cogent replies by defenders of such a notion. And (4) the petitionary prayer argument will only be impressive to those who agree with me that the sorts of petitions I listed make sense, and few believers in limited Gods will so agree.

Nevertheless, I am prepared to defend each of the above four ways of arguing on behalf of an unlimited God. The notion of an unlimited God is, I believe, the best way of capturing what Christians find about God both in scripture and in the tradition. Such a notion is impressively supported by the ontological argument. It is at least indirectly supported by difficulties that plague limited God theologies. And it, unlike them, seems religiously adequate. My recommendation is that Christians continue to affirm that God is unlimited.[14]

Notes

1.   See *Encountering Evil*, ed. by Stephen T. Davis (Atlanta: John Knox Press, 1981) p. 118.

2. Richard Swinburne, *The Existence of God* (Oxford: The Clarendon Press, 1979) pp. 93–5, 282–3.

3. Saint Anselm, *Basic Writings* (La Salle, Illinois: Open Court, 1962) p. 7.

4. It began with a paper in graduate school on 'Kant and the Ontological Argument' (unpublished). Others include: 'Anselm and Gaunilo on the "Lost Island" ', *The Southern Journal of Philosophy*, Vol. XIII (Winter 1975) No. 4, and four articles in the *International Journal for Philosophy of Religion*: 'Does the Ontological Argument Beg the Question?', Vol. VII (Winter 1976) No. 4, 'Anselm and Question-Begging: A Reply to William Rowe', Vol. VII (Winter 1976) No. 4, 'Loptson on Anselm and Rowe', Vol. XIII (1982) No. 4, and 'Loptson on Anselm and Davis', Vol. XVI (1984) No. 3.

5. For a helpful explication of the concept, see *The Nature of Necessity*, by Alvin Plantinga (Oxford: Clarendon Press, 1974) Ch. I.

6. Anselm occasionally uses the term *melius* ('better') instead of *maius* 'greater'. See also *Monologion* II and *Proslogion* V (where he says to God: 'Therefore, thou art just, truthful, blessed, and whatever it is better to be than not to be').

7. I am ignoring the various recent attempts to show that the theistic concept of God is incoherent – for example, that omniscience is incompatible with immutability, that omnipotence is incompatible with perfect goodness, that incorporeality is incompatible with agency and so on. All such attempts, in my opinion, have been shown to fail.

8. Tom Morris, 'The God of Abraham, Isaac, and Anselm', *Faith and Philosophy*, Vol. 1 (April 1984) No. 2.

9. See the Appendix for a formalized statement of this version of OA. (It should be noted that while I claim to have presented a valid version of the OA, I have not tried to defend it against the various questions that have been raised about its deep structure, for instance, whether 'exists' is a predicate or property, whether the basic form of the argument can be used to 'prove' the existence of other entities beside the GCB, whether the OA makes illicit assumptions about non-existing objects or non-referring singular terms, or whether the OA begs the question.) A possible difficulty should be briefly noted here as well. On the second definition of the term 'unlimited being' mentioned above (see p. 5), there are unlimited beings who could have been greater than they are – their G-properties that admit of no intrinsic maximum are always going to be conceivably possessed to a greater degree than they in fact are. But this turns out not to be a problem since I define the term 'greatest conceivable being' only in terms of a G-property (viz. omnipotence) that *does* admit of an intrinsic maximum.

10. It emerges clearly, I believe, in discussion of David Griffin's theodicy in *Encountering Evil*.

11. Thus David Griffin: 'The doctrine of omnipotence is not based upon historical revelation, but upon imaginative flights designed to fulfill egocentric wishes'. *Ibid.*, p. 132.

12. *Ibid.*, p. 130.
13. See J. N. Findlay, 'Can God's Existence Be Disproved?' in A. Flew and A. MacIntyre, *New Essays in Philosophical Theology* (New York: Macmillan, 1955) pp. 47–56.
14. I would like to thank Professors John Hick, Charles Young and Linda Zagzebski for their helpful suggestions on an earlier draft of this chapter.

Appendix

What follows is a formalized statement of the version of the OA that I am defending. As with any attempt to put a concrete argument into symbols, some nuances are slightly different than the verbal version in the main body of the paper. First some definitions:

(1) Let 'G' be an individual constant meaning 'the greatest conceivable being';
(2) Let 'E' be a predicate constant meaning 'exists in reality';
(3) Let 'e' be a predicate constant meaning 'exists in the mind';
(4) Let '>AB' be a function meaning 'A is greater than B';
(5) Let 'λ' be a variable ranging over levels of greatness;
(6) Let 'Λ' be a singular term refering to a particular level of greatness with the term following it indicating the level (so that 'ΛA' means 'the level of greatness of A');
(7) Let 'Lp' mean '(the proposition) p is necessarily true'; and
(8) Let 'Mp' mean '(the proposition) p is possibly true'.

The rest of the notation is fairly standard.

(1)	L(x)[(Ex & ex) v (Ex & ~ex) v (~Ex & ex) v (~Ex & ~ex)]	A
(2)	L[(EG & eG) v (EG & ~eG) v (~EG & eG) v (~EG & ~eG)]	(1), UI
(3)	(EG & eG) v (EG & ~eG) v (~EG & eG) v (~EG & ~eG)	(2), Axiom of necessity
(4)	eG	A
(5)	(EG & eG) v (~EG & eG)	(3), (4) VE
(6)	M(EG)	A
(7)	L(x) [(ex & ~Ex & M(Ex))→ M(∃λ) λ>Λ x]	A
(8)	L[(eG & ~EG & M(EG))→M(∃λ) λ>Λ G]	(7), UI
(9)	[eG & ~EG & M(EG)]→M(∃λ) λ>Λ G	(8), Axiom of necessity
(10)	eG & ~EG	A (premise for RAA)
(11)	eG & ~EG & M(EG)	(10), (6), & I
(12)	M(∃λ) λ>Λ G	(9), (11), MPP
(13)	L(x)[(M(∃λ) λ>Λ x)→M (∃y) (>yx)]	A
(14)	L[(M(∃λ) λ>Λ G)→M(∃y)(>yG)]	(13), UI

(15) M(∃λ) λ>Λ G→M(∃y)(>yG)   (14), Axiom of necessity
(16) M(∃y) (>yG)   (12), (15) MPP
(17) M(∃y) (>yG)→G≠ G   (16), Df. of 'G'
(18) G ≠ G   (16), (17), MPP
(19) ~(~EG & eG)   (10), (18), RAA
(20) EG & eG   (5), (19) VE

2

Reply: Must God Be Unlimited? Naturalistic vs. Supernaturalistic Theism

David Ray Griffin

Stephen Davis, in arguing that God must be unlimited, is arguing primarily against the God of process theology. He claims to be opposing to this view the 'God of classical Christian theism, that is, the God of Augustine, Aquinas, Calvin, Barth, *et al.*' However, the God of those theologians is considerably different from the being Davis portrays. For example, Davis believes that God could exercise all the power in the universe but has chosen not to do so, giving instead some power of self-determination to human beings (EE, 127).[1] God's omnipotence is God's ability to control all events, but this is an ability that God does not always exercise. But Calvin explicitly rejected this notion of divine omnipotence as an ability to do all things which sometimes 'sits idle'; he ridiculed the distinction between God's doing and God's mere permission, 'as if God sat in a watchtower awaiting chance events, and his judgment thus depended upon human will' (*Institutes,* I.xvi.3; I.xviii.1; see GPE, 116–18). Aquinas insists that God is *actus purus*, which means that there can be no unactualized potency in God. Aquinas also insists upon God's simplicity, which means that there can be no distinction between the various divine attributes, such as God's knowledge and causation. Hence, contrary to Davis's view, for Aquinas as well as for Calvin, for God to know something is for God to cause it.

However, although Davis's position does not articulate the theism of the classical Christian theologians, it does enunciate the popular supernaturalistic theism which has probably been the dominant view among ordinary Christians, and which is also the view attacked by most agnostics in the West. Because Davis is 'an analytic philosopher, trained in logic and twentieth-century linguistic philosophy' (EE, 69), and attempts to use these sophisticated tools to defend the view of God held by the majority of less sophisticated believers, his position is worth taking seriously. If his defence is unsuccessful, that would be good reason for less philosophically trained adherents of popular supernaturalism to consider other possible ways to conceive of the Holy Power of the universe to which we owe our existence and in whose power lies our ultimate hope.

The way I recommend is just that approach which Davis attacks, that of process theology. The differences between this theology and Davis's can best be summarized as the distinction between naturalistic and supernaturalistic theism. As naturalistic theists, process theologians hold that *the existence of a realm of finite beings with power is not a contingent, arbitrary fact, based upon a divine decision*. The *form* our particular world has taken is contingent and is basically due to God's creative activity. But the *existence* of a realm of finite actualities is as eternal and necessary as the existence of God, and to be 'actual' means to embody some creativity or energy with which to exercise self-determination and causal influence upon others. Also, there are some necessary (metaphysical) principles descriptive of the possibilities for causal interaction among these finite actualities, and between these actualities and God. The most fundamental 'laws of nature' were not imposed on the world by God but are eternal features of reality. Accordingly, the basic relation between God and the world is not due to an arbitrary divine decision but belongs to the eternal and hence necessary features of reality.

Process theologians accordingly do not believe that the basic causal relations of the world can be interrupted from time to time, or that we can look forward to a time when the basic structure of existence will be suddenly and radically changed. Not believing in a supernaturalistic creation, process theologians also do not believe in supernatural miracles or supernatural scriptures protected from human fallibility; nor do we hope for a supernatural eschaton. To call this view 'naturalistic' does not mean that process theologians do not believe in God's efficacy in the world; but it means that this efficacy never involves a unilateral interruption of the powers of and causal relations between the creatures. God is limited in what God can do by the causal power of the other actualities.

Given this characterization of naturalistic theism, Davis's view is thoroughly supernaturalistic. He believes that God created our world *ex nihilo*, in the sense of absolute nothingness (EE, 126); that it is possible for God to have all the power in the universe and that we have power only because God freely chose to give some to us (EE, 127); that God's power is not essentially limited by the power of any other actualities, so that God can control all other beings; that the 'causal laws' of nature were imposed on the world by God[2]; that God can accordingly interrupt the normal causal patterns of the world, thereby unilaterally healing diseases, deflecting speeding bullets and automobiles, parting waters, raising the dead, and preventing the world's destruction (EE, 127); that God has inspired the Bible in such a way that it can be used as an external guarantee for the truth of certain doctrines (EE, 127). And Davis's theodicy depends upon the expectation that God will someday use the divine omnipotence, which has been held in reserve, to overcome evil and redeem the world (EE, 71, 79, 82f., 93, 95, 121–8). Since Davis accepts a supernaturalist doctrine of creation, according to which the existence of finite beings and the causal laws obtaining among them were unilaterally determined by God, it is consistent for him to believe that God can unilaterally intervene in the world to bring about certain effects now and then and that God will unilaterally bring about an eschaton in which the evil-producing factors in our present situation will be completely abolished.

Naturalistic and supernaturalistic theism both agree, against naturalistic atheism, that there is an actuality distinct from the totality of finite things worthy of worship and hence of the name 'God' – a purposive being perfect in power and goodness, who is the world's creator and is presently active in it. Nevertheless, naturalistic theism is as different from supernaturalistic theism as it is from naturalistic atheism. The opposition between the two views comes to a head regarding the issue on which Davis focuses: must God be unlimited? Is the supernaturalistic conception of God the only one worthy of the name 'God'? There is a large consensus, among theists and atheists alike, that the word 'God' does refer to a being with the kind of power that Davis ascribes to the greatest possible being. However, naturalistic theists (along with many atheists, who use this as their chief argument against theism) believe that the un-limited being of which supernaturalists speak is not a possible being at all. Hence, naturalistic theists hold that God not only *need not* but also *must not* be thought to be unlimited.

Davis suggests four arguments for the unlimited God of super-naturalism and hence against the God of naturalistic theism. How-ever, these arguments finally reduce to one: that the concept of a being that is unlimited (except by logical impossibilities, which is no limitation at all) is a coherent notion. That is the crucial issue involved in the ontological argument[3] which is the focus of Davis's second argument. That the notion of an unlimited being is indeed coherent is the basis for the conclusion of his argument that the God of process theology is not worthy of worship, since it is not the greatest conceivable being. The point of the fourth argument is essentially the same. Davis's first argument, that pertinent statements in the Bible can be accepted as revelatory of God's unlimited power, presupposes the coherence of the idea of a God who can infallibly inspire a book. Hence the twofold point to examine is the coherence of this notion of an unlimited being and Davis's treatment of process theology's arguments against its coherence.

Davis realizes that the challenge to the coherence of the idea of an unlimited God is the chief one his view faces. At one place he says that he is going to ignore recent attempts to show that the traditional concept of God as an unlimited being is incoherent. However, that should not be seen as a sign that Davis takes the issue of coherence to be unimportant; rather, he ignores those attempts, for the purposes of this chapter, because he believes they have failed. If he thought they had succeeded, he would, according to his own principles, have to reject that notion of God, since it would be as ruled out by logic as are square circles. Indeed, he rejects Descartes' doctrine of divine omnipotence on this basis. And he expressly promises to take up the claim by process theologians in particular that the view of God as unlimited is incoherent.

However, his actual treatment of this issue is disappointing. In an earlier exchange, Davis had asked for arguments as to why I thought the traditional doctrine of omnipotence incoherent (EE, 127). I referred him to the places where those arguments could be found, then added an additional one (EE, 130). In his present chapter, Davis ignores all but the additional argument, and he distorts that one.

That additional argument begins with 'a fundamental fact of the empirical situation' which is that all actualities seem to have self-determining power which cannot be totally overridden. The suggestion of process theology is that this experienced fact about our world be assumed to be a metaphysical or necessary fact, one that would hold in any world God could create. This is of course an unprovable speculative hypothesis. But the contrary idea that there could be a world with creatures totally devoid of self-determining power is at least equally speculative. In fact – and this is the main point – it is even more speculative, since it is devoid of any experiential grounding. We have no experience of a world totally devoid of freedom or self-determining power. We thereby have no experiential basis for knowing that such a world is even possible. Accordingly, process theology's hypothesis that the power of creatures to deviate from the will of their creator is a necessary truth is much less speculative than Davis's hypothesis that there could be a world in which God would have all the power. Should there not be a presumption in favour of the less speculative hypothesis so that the burden of proof is on those who plump for the more speculative one?

Davis's treatment of this argument distorts it beyond recognition. First, he says that my argument is to 'simply assume' that the truth that we have power is a necessary truth, failing to mention that this was an additional supplementary argument. Second, he then asks: 'Is it helpful to take contingent truths and suppose that they are necessary truths?' *Of course* that would not be helpful, since it would be self-contradictory; a contingent truth cannot also be a necessary truth. Davis's question arises only because he has made the question-begging assumption that the power of creatures to act contrary to God's will is a contingent truth, in the same class as the existence of kangaroos.

Process theology has a number of interlocking arguments for believing the notion of an unlimited God (in Davis's sense) to be as incoherent as that of a square circle. Because it is incoherent, it provides no standard against which to judge the God of process theology to be imperfect in power and hence less great than the greatest conceivable being. Hence we do not say, as Davis suggests, that the problem of evil can be solved only if God is 'sufficiently impotent' or 'weak enough' to be incapable of unilaterally preventing evil. That way of putting it begs the question. Process theologians agree that God must be thought of as the greatest possible being and that this includes having perfect power; it even involves being the ultimately decisive power in reality (GPE, 268ff.; EE, 117, 133). But we maintain that the greatest conceivable or possible power does not involve the power unilaterally to prevent evil. It would make sense to call the God of process theology 'weak' or 'impotent' only if a being with greater power were a coherent notion, and that is what we deny.

These arguments about power do not exhaust process theologians' reasons for considering supernaturalism incoherent. There are many others. For example, there is the incoherence involved in the conjunction of human freedom and divine foreknowledge (or timeless omniscience, if God be regarded as outside of time). Even if one denies the Thomistic notion of divine simplicity, so that one can say that God knows the future (that is, the events that are still future for us) without thereby causing it, it seems self-contradictory to say that these divinely known acts are free. Davis agrees, I believe, that being free in a sense that makes us somewhat responsible for our actions involves a capacity to choose among alternative possibilities. An act was not free unless we could have done otherwise. But if God, whose knowledge is infallible, knows (whether 'eternally' or with 'foreknowledge') that we will do X at a particular time, it is impossible that we could do Y or Z. If Davis cannot show his idea of God to be coherent, the high regard he claims to have for rationality, and in particular for coherence, would seem to require that he give up that idea of God.

As can be seen in earlier discussions, however, serious questions about the overall coherence of his position do not shake him. He tends to respond to all potentially embarrassing questions by saying, 'I just don't know'.[4] Some of the questions for which he makes this plea are: why God created beings he knew would be damned; why God created moral monsters; why God did not intervene to prevent the holocaust; why God does not prevent natural evils (EE, 81, 95, 97). These points seem to critics to imply incoherencies in the view that this world is the creation of a being unlimited in power and goodness. But Davis, while saying that he would reject classical theism if it could be shown to be incoherent, retains the privilege of calling all apparent incoherencies mere 'mysteries', about which we should trust God, and not 'question him inordinately' (EE, 82–3).

Davis's cavalier dismissal of all such difficulties suggests that reason does not play as important a role in his outlook as he suggests. Rather, revelation is more important. The main reason for believing that God must be unlimited seems to be that the Bible authoritatively contains God's self-revelation of this truth. As Davis says, he approaches the problem of evil 'with certain beliefs already intact' (EE, 92). Accordingly, his only question is whether it is rational for him to retain these beliefs (*ibid*.). And by being 'rational' he means only being able to see that none of his beliefs are strictly self-contradictory; he does not mean being able to develop a view that can convince others that his outlook is probable, or even plausible (EE, 77, 79).

Indeed, Davis distinguishes between the 'logical problem of evil' and the 'emotive problem of evil'. Under the latter come questions about the plausibility or probability of his view. In other words, the *philosophical* aspect of the problem is reduced to showing that his position cannot be proved to be logically inconsistent. All questions about the probability or plausibility of his view are reduced to 'emotive' difficulties. These difficulties create 'evangelistic' difficulties, he grants, but these difficulties in getting other people to believe his position are not problems for him to deal with *qua* philosopher (EE, 77, 79). The difficulties arise because the solutions depend on propositions that 'are only known by revelation'. Accordingly, one needs to appeal to 'private evidence'. There is no apparent way for these propositions to 'be substantiated by means of public evidence' (EE, 80).

We must take this into account in evaluating Davis's claim that God must be unlimited. Davis's chapter 1 has the appearance of being a public argument. Although he mentions that one could bolster the argument by appeals to Biblical revelation, he appears not to rest much of the weight of his argument on this basis, since the Bible is open to multiple interpretations, and some people do not consider it an external guarantee of the truth of particular doctrines. He then appears to move to public arguments for the proposition that God must be unlimited. However, if a *public argument* is one that attempts to show that one view is more plausible than another on the basis of public evidence, Davis is decidedly not offering public arguments. He is only offering *in public* his rationale for being able to hold on to a particular view of God even though its plausibility cannot be publicly defended. Hence, Davis is not offering any publicly defensible reasons for believing that God must, or even can, be unlimited. He is only offering in public the private reasons why he and other like-minded supernaturalists think the creator of the world can and must be an unlimited being.

What then is the status of Davis's claim that God cannot be limited? His argument against the God of process theology is that it is not as great as the God of supernaturalism. This criticism translates pragmatically into the complaint that the God of process theology cannot unilaterally grant all of our petitions; it is 'just not able to do all the things asked for'. If God cannot unilaterally heal us from all forms of disease and unilaterally prevent the world's destruction,[5] then this putative God 'is not God, or at least is not worthy of the worship, love, and obedience Christians believe we owe God'. The message about a God who cannot unilaterally do such things is not gospel: 'There is no good news in the news that God is trying very hard and just might succeed'. But Davis is by implication saying: 'It is better news that the universe is under the control of a being who could have prevented Hiroshima and Auschwitz, but chose not to; who could have prevented the suffering of starving children throughout the world, but chose not to; who could have prevented the extermination of Native Americans, and the enslavement of Blacks in America and South Africa, but chose not to; who could have prevented the occurrence of such diseases as cancer, AIDS, and mental retardation, but chose not to. Your life is in the control of such a being. Rejoice!' In comparison with such a 'gospel', is it such bad news to hear that the creator of our universe, who had the power to bring creatures such as us out of nucleons and electrons, is totally *for* us, constantly seeking our wholeness, but that whether we realize that wholeness is finally up to the way we respond?

It is clear that the God of supernaturalism can do all sorts of things unilaterally that the God of naturalistic theism can only do if the creatures freely co-operate. Whether this makes the God of supernaturalism more worthy of worship[6] is, I have suggested, at best a moot point, even assuming the coherence of the supernaturalistic conception. But that latter point is the basic one. Supernaturalists cannot meaningfully call other conceptions 'religiously inadequate' by comparison with a conception that is philosophically incoherent since the fundamental criterion for judging a conception religiously adequate is precisely that it be the conception of a being greater than which none other is *coherently* conceivable.

Notes

1. The initials EE stand for *Encountering Evil: Live Options in Theodicy*, ed. Stephen T. Davis (John Knox, 1981); GPE stands for my *God, Power, and Evil: A Process Theodicy* (Westminster, 1976).
2. Instead of denying that God is limited by the power of the creatures, Davis speaks instead of the 'causal laws' (2, 19), which is the characteristic language of those who think of the laws of nature as rules imposed from without, as opposed to thinking sociologically of the so-called laws of nature as really being the 'habits of nature'.
3. I pass over here most of the possible problems in the version of the ontological argument which he defends. I make only two comments.

David Ray Griffin

31

First, it is the version which Hartshorne, Norman Malcolm and many others consider invalid. Second, the idea that 'concepts presumably have some abilities', being different only in degree from actual things, is strange. It renders any argument dependent upon it almost certainly unsound. It supports my view that logical arguments about the real world inevitably presuppose metaphysical judgements. The notion that 'metaphysical' philosophy can be eschewed in favour of purely 'analytical' philosophy usually just leads to *bad* metaphysics. See my 'Actuality, Possibility, and Theodicy: A Response to Nelson Pike', *Process Studies* 12/3 (Autumn 1982) 168–79, esp. 170–2.

4. John Roth has charged him with relying basically upon an 'I Just Don't Know Defense' (EE, 90).

5. Davis listed two other types of petition God must be able (unilaterally) to grant: one is the petition for forgiveness of sins. This need not be discussed, since that is precisely the type of petition God *can* unilaterally grant. The other is the petition for continued life beyond bodily death. I have already said that I believe God to have the kind of power needed to renew our lives beyond bodily death (EE, 135; GPE, 311, 313). I simply do not believe that this renewal requires unilateral omnipotence.

6. Davis says that the basic question facing process theologians, which in his view 'has never been solved', is whether their God of limited power is 'worthy of our worship'. I did devote an entire chapter, entitled 'Worshipfulness and the Omnipotence Fallacy', to this topic in *God, Power, and Evil*.

3

Comment on Stephen Davis

John Hick

Davis's paper has the clarity that enables discussion of it to be profitable. I want to suggest that his version of the ontological argument fails for the reason that has so often been pointed out in relation to Anselm's argument in *Proslogion* II, with which it is (as Davis himself notes) virtually identical. It goes wrong at the beginning, in proposition 1, 'Things can exist in only two ways, in the mind and in reality'. The familiar objection, classically formulated by Kant and with its central principle reformulated by Russell in his theory of descriptions, is that talk of things existing in the mind, and of some of them (for instance, unicorns) existing only in the mind whilst others (for instance lions) exist also in reality, is a precritical way of saying that some of our concepts (for instance, 'lion') have instances whilst others (for instance, 'unicorn') do not. To say that lions exist, or that there are lions, is to say that the concept 'lion' is instantiated; and to say that unicorns do not exist is to say that the concept 'unicorn' is uninstantiated. Thus instead of beginning with the affirmation that the GCB (greatest conceivable being) exists in the mind, and that the question is whether it also exists in reality, we should say that we have the concept 'GCB', and the question is whether it is instantiated. This familiar modern objection to things-existing-in-the-mind language is relevant directly or indirectly to each of Davis's propositions.

From the illegitimate proposition 'The GCB exists in the mind' it was possible to argue (with Anselm and Davis) that in order to be the *greatest* conceivable being the GCB must exist in reality also. But from the legitimate proposition 'We have the concept of the "GCB"', it is not possible to argue that this concept, in order to be the concept of the greatest conceivable being, must be instantiated. The concept of the GCB is still a concept, and whether or not it is instantiated is a further factual question. This cannot be decided *a priori*, or by definition, but only *a posteriori*, by some kind of procedure of observation or experience.

Davis's argument is not helped, but only slightly obscured, by substituting for the GCB existing in the mind the GCB as a 'possible existing thing' which exists as 'a set of compossible properties'. This more exotic animal is simply the possibly instantiated concept of 'the GCB' in fancy dress. But we can see through the fancy dress to the precritical imposter beneath it!

4

Response to John Hick

Stephen T. Davis

It is unclear to me precisely how the Kant–Russell line of argument shows that my version of the OA breaks down – that is, is either formally invalid, informally invalid, or unsound. Nevertheless, the thrust of Hick's objection is clear – it is illicit and precritical to speak, as the OA does, of existence 'in the mind'.

Now I am unconvinced by Kant's influential claim in the *First Critique* that 'exists' is not a 'real predicate'. At times this is surely true, as in the following dialogue:

Do you have a pencil?
Yes, I do.
Is your pencil yellow?
Yes.
Is there an eraser on your pencil?
Yes.
But does your pencil exist?

The problem here is that the pencil's existence was apparently presupposed throughout the conversation; thus the oddness of the concluding question. If the reply to it were, 'Yes, my pencil does indeed exist', this would not (as Kant would say) *change* or *expand* our concept of the pencil. Here Kant is right. But in those cases where the existence of a thing is not necessarily assumed, to say that it exists might well expand our concept of it. My concept of the Loch Ness monster would change if you were to convince me that the creature exists. Here 'exists' can be a real predicate.

But the deep issue between Hick and me concerns talk of existence 'in the mind'. I see no fatal problem here; exactly why is it 'pre-critical'? (Such talk certainly would be illegitimate if the claim that something exists in the mind were covertly taken to entail some other, more substantial, species of existence; but it is not.) Nor do I

34

agree that 'x exists in the mind' is just a different way of saying what we can more felicitously express by talk of uninstantiated concepts. If it were merely a matter of saying the same thing in more currently permissible words, then the OA could equally well be expressed in the terminology Hick allows. But if Hick is right that it can't, then there is a substantive metaphysical claim (viz., 'there are no property-bearing non-existent things') buried in Hick's apparently merely linguistic point.

I think it makes perfectly good sense to speak of possibly existing things (that is, sets of compossible properties that might exist in reality) and to say that a possibly existing thing that exists in reality is greater (in the sense defined in my chapter) than that thing would be if it did not exist in reality. If I am right, the Kant-Russell argument does not refute the OA.

Finally, it begs the question against the OA to insist that you cannot prove the existence of the GCB by purely *a priori* means. The OA purports to be a counter-example to the general principle presupposed here (viz., that only by probabilistic appeals to experience can the existence of a thing be proved). That the OA is not a counter-example to this principle must be shown by an internal critique of the OA itself, not simply by insisting that what it tries to do cannot be done.

Part II

5

A Process Concept of God

John B. Cobb, Jr.

My primary self-definition is as a theologian. Dealing with the concept of God as a theologian, one is always in the midst of a discussion, a discussion that is continuous with that reflected in the Bible. Most of the time that is the way I deal with the question of God intellectually.

Nevertheless, there is another approach, and in a discussion on philosophy of religion it seems an appropriate one. That approach is to simplify and formalize one's way of raising the question of God and to give it a systematic character it never actually has in the course of life. I shall try to do that here.

That decision prepares the way for another. Shall I begin by defining what I mean by God and then compare this with reality to determine its applicability? Or shall I begin with an analysis of the most general features of reality to determine whether it is appropriate to call any of them God. I will follow the second approach. Not that in fact I have ever thought in a way so neutral to the inherited faith in God! Nor that the analysis I offer will in fact be independent of that faith! But there is some value in presenting the analysis as if it were more independent than it is. I hardly need to add that my analysis and judgements are also profoundly indebted to Alfred North Whitehead, and this relation I shall make quite explicit.

I

There are many starting points for analyzing the most general features of reality. The choice again has arbitrary elements. I have chosen to begin by describing a view widespread in secular circles and explaining why I feel the need for supplementation.

The account of reality with which I begin is a simple one. Individual philosophers add rich detail, but that is not important for my purposes. The situation is one in which there are events, and there is an interest in explaining them. Why does the car not start? Why did the temperature of the room rise by ten degrees? Why does light curve? Why does the caged tiger pace back and forth? Why does the boy lash out at his mother?

These questions require careful formulation. We must be clear just which features of an event we are seeking to explain. Then we must describe the initial conditions, namely, the situation out of which the event occurred. In the view I am describing, the explanation must be found somewhere in those conditions.

We can speak of the aspect of these conditions, or the complex of aspects, explanatory of the feature in question as its cause. However, this introduces many puzzles, and it is not necessary to introduce the notion of 'cause' to make my point. It is enough to say that the feature is explained by aspects of its initial conditions. These precede the feature to be explained.

Many philosophers believe that every feature of the event in question can be explained in this way. Given the conditions from which the event arose, every feature must be as it in fact is. This is the doctrine of determinism. Some determinists emphasize that among the conditions in which the full explanation is sought, some of the most important are the desires, plans and intelligent reflections of actors. These thinkers are called 'soft determinists'. But since these conditions always antedate what is to be explained, and since they in their turn can be exhaustively explained by their antecedents, soft determinism remains a form of determinism.

Some philosophers allow for an element of indeterminism. They may or may not be influenced in this regard by the role of indeterminism in physics. Indeterminism can be derived from the fact that any event is inexhaustibly complex. No matter how many of its features are explained, the event as a whole in its actual concreteness can never be exhaustively explained. There is always an element of chance.

Now what are the implications of these positions? The implications in which I am most interested are those having to do with human experience. What happens to human responsibility? My judgement is that it disappears. I realize that interesting theories have been devised to show that determinism (and/or indeterminism) is compatible with the reality of human responsibility. It would be interesting to discuss those theories in detail. But I am simply reporting on my conviction, which also has much support in the literature. If I were persuaded that in every moment all that occurred in my experience were predetermined – or that what was not predetermined occurred by chance – I would regard my sense of being responsible for my actions as illusory. But I do not in fact regard this as illusory. Hence I have to believe that there is something missing in this picture of reality. Indeed, I believe quite a lot is missing. Let us explore the event further.

II

The account above focused on features of events that distinguish them one from the other and asked for their efficient causes. We could also ask why any event occurs at all, or what ultimately is the nature of events, or why do the features of one event find their explanation in antecedent ones. These are metaphysical questions, and a great deal of ingenuity has been employed in showing them to be meaningless. But in one form or another the questions persist.

My own judgement is that one of the most important and inescapable metaphysical questions is that which presses the question for the material cause. Few deny that it is meaningful to ask the question of the material cause of a piece of paper; that is, of what is it composed? When the answer is given in chemical terms, one can press for the physical components. Eventually one will arrive at the electromagnetic events or at some still more fundamental field. Here, or at some point further on, the question changes its character. Down to that point the answer is in terms of component parts that, like the entities of which they are parts, have both form or structure and constituent parts. But at some point one has arrived at an entity that has no components. It has, of course, a form. But *of what* is it a form?

In much of our tradition the answer would have been prime matter. Einstein spoke of matter-energy. Others prefer to speak simply of energy. In the great religio-metaphysical traditions other terms have been used. Brahman, Emptiness, and Being Itself are among the answers. Whitehead spoke of creativity.

Whatever name one gives, and whether one approaches it as a physicist, a metaphysician or a mystic, some commonalities emerge. All recognize that one cannot speak of this as one speaks of all the things and events that instantiate it. It has no form or qualities. None of the ordinary language developed to speak of particulars, or of classes, or of abstractions applies to this. It is not actual, because it is actuality–itself. It is not real, because it is reality-itself. It does not exist, because it is existence-itself. It is not a being because it is being-itself. It is not dynamic because it is dynamism-itself. It is not creative, because it is creativity-itself.

I will not press the matter further. I have come only to the beginning of metaphysical discussion. I am convinced that discussion is valid and needed, despite its difficulties. I am convinced also that those who have through generations developed the art of realizing Brahman or Emptiness in their own experience have much to teach those for whom the approach has been primarily conceptual.

III

My foray into metaphysics is important for expanding the picture of the situation. But it does not take me far toward the understanding of personal responsibility. The metaphysical reality of which I have been speaking is beyond all categories of good and evil, better and worse, right and wrong. What it contributes lies in a different direction. Yet my sense of responsibility remains. What would have to be the case for it to be valid?

Three things seem necessary. There would have to be alternatives. Some alternatives would have to be better than others. There would have to be self-determination in the event itself as to which alternative is selected. Because responsibility seems real to me, I am pressed to affirm these preconditions. But how can they be true?

The event now under consideration is a moment of my own personal experience. That much of it is the outcome of the past goes without saying. The question is whether it is exhaustively so, or whether its inexhaustibility points to an element of indeterminism or chance, or whether there is a real element of self-determination within the moment itself. The sense of responsibility argues for this latter, but how is it possible? Self-determination would have to be determination among alternative ways of responding to the determining power of the past or of supplementing what in the event is determined by the past. This would require that the event be constituted not only by its relation to the past world but also by a relation to alternative relevant possibilities for its own self-constitution. Finally, these possibilities must be graded in value.

The realization of some must be objectively better than the realization of others. Otherwise the self-determination is pointless.

As I examine my experience these requirements all seem to be met. I do have a sense of choosing among real alternative ways of constituting myself or my experience. I do have a sense of being called or drawn toward preferable alternatives, sometimes against the resistance of my habits. Phenomenologically the requirements for true responsibility are present. Is there any justification, nevertheless, for denying the reality?

So far as I can tell the chief justification is implicitly metaphysical. Many assume that there can be nothing out of which the new event can be constituted except the initial conditions. Nothing arises from nothing. Hence any sense of alternatives among which one chooses must arise out of these initial conditions and be explained by them. The alternatives sensed must themselves be explained from these initial conditions, as well as the 'decision' among them. Hence there are no real alternatives, and there is no real choice.

Another theory is possible. There might be in the totality of reality an agency of possibility that supplements the many agencies of necessity. There might be an activity that brings into relevance to the initial conditions possibilities for including in the new event something not derived from those conditions. This metaphysical belief accords more closely with experience phenomenologically considered than does the other. If correspondence with pervasive experience is an important consideration in choosing metaphysics, as I believe, then it is better to affirm this. I do affirm it.

IV

I have sketched some reasons for making two metaphysical moves from the initial situation of an event and its antecedent conditions. One move is toward the ultimate reality of which it is an instantiation. The other move is toward a principle or agency of possibility through which self-determination becomes real in at least some events. The question now is, has either move anything to do with God? And at this point we must ask what that word, minimally, means.

If 'God' is taken to mean a Supreme Person, radically transcendent of the universe, by whose will all things happen as they do, then it would seem that the discussion to date is quite irrelevant to belief in

God or even counts against it. If by 'God' is meant Ultimate Reality, whatever that turns out to be, then the first metaphysical move is highly promising, and to learn more of God we should proceed with the inquiry there initiated. If, on the other hand, by 'God' is meant a gracious agency worthy of trust and worship, then the second move is more promising. This is the direction Whitehead pursued, and I have followed him.

Whether the two metaphysical moves I have proposed are justified is open to discussion. I certainly do not conceive that I have proved that there is an ultimate material cause or a principle of possibility. I do find myself thinking in these terms, and I have tried to show how I come to these convictions through reflections that are relatively independent from my Christian faith. My further discussion presupposes these first steps.

But whereas those steps may be right or wrong and the affirmations resultant from them true or false, once they are taken the choice with respect to the use of the word 'God' is not. There is no one correct way to use it. The word has diverse minimal meanings among believers and unbelievers alike. All of the three meanings I have mentioned are possible ones, along with many others. The decision among them may be made with some detachment, attempting to assess how the word is most commonly used. Or the decision can be made with existential passion, as in my case, because of the nature of one's deepest concern. To me the question of whether there is anything or anyone which or whom I can wholly trust is a fundamental one, more urgent than the question of 'ultimate reality', interesting though that is. I cannot separate my use of 'God' from this sense of importance.

There is another criterion for using the term 'God' that is important to those of us who are Christians. That is its continuity with the use of the word in the church and especially in the Bible. Judgements about such continuity may be right or wrong, although decisions are certainly difficult. There is rich diversity in the tradition, and most of the past conceptualities are bound up with worldviews that are now obsolete. There will be inevitable discontinuities as well as continuities. Still, I am prepared to argue that my choice is the more suitable one for the sake of appropriate continuity, although I am not sure I could do this apart from some further development of my understanding of this agency of possibility and self-determination, of freedom and responsibility.

V

My next step in reflecting about this agency is to follow Whitehead in his ontological principle. This principle is that only actual entities can act. To be an agency is to be an actual entity. It follows that the agency creative of freedom is an actual entity.

This actual entity is different from other actual entities. It mediates to us possibilities rather than exercising physical compulsion upon us. Also it endures everlastingly rather than existing but a moment as do actual occasions. It is immediately present to all actual occasions rather than being spatially located at one point. Many of the traditional doctrines about God and creatures reappear in these reflections.

But the fact that what I shall now, without further apology, call God is, like all real individuals, an actual entity, does enable us to ask about similarities as well as contrasts. The most important of these at this stage of the development of the doctrine is that God is, like all other actual entities, di-polar.

I can explain di-polarity in general by reference back to the situation described above. The new actual occasion of my experience was largely shaped by the causal efficacy of the other occasions constituting its initial conditions. In Whitehead's vocabulary it physically felt these initial data. It conformed to them of necessity. That is, they imposed themselves upon it. Whatever belongs to the physical aspect or pole of an occasion can be explained just as the determinists say. But there was another pole to the occasion made possible by God. In this pole possibilities were experienced and compared in various ways with actuality. A decision was made by the occasion as to how to constitute itself. The decisions for the occasion by past occasions were supplemented by the occasion's own decision as to what to be for its future. This supplementary and creative activity of an occasion is its mental pole. The occasions of human experience begin physically and complete themselves mentally.

Now God has been introduced as the agency that makes available to the occasions possibilities relevant to their situations. This accents the 'mental' character of God. All possibilities exist in and for God and are ordered by God in relation to the world. God seems to be purely mental. That would mean that God acts on the world but is not affected by the world. This doctrine would have affinities with much in the tradition. It is a suggestive direction for speculation.

But Whitehead chose the alternative speculation. He proposed that God, like all other actual entities, is di-polar, that is, possesses both a mental and a physical pole. To put this in another way, he concluded that the world acts upon God as God acts upon the world. Much of what is most interesting in Whitehead's doctrine of God, and most widely characteristic of process theology, depends upon this move. Does this speculation have sufficient warrant?

Part of the reason for positing a physical pole in God is the strong sense of interrelatedness of things that pervades Whitehead's thought. He did not want to interrupt this principle short of God. He also believed, and I agree, that this idea fits with some elements of religious experience, namely, those in which God is experienced more personally. Also, if God is only mental, unaffected by the world, the decision of God ordering possibilities in their relation to the actual world has to be seen as a single primordial decision made without reference to the actual character of the world. If, on the other hand, God experiences the world, then the decision can be an ongoing one, responsive to what is happening in the world. There are conceptual advantages in this view, and it too makes contact with some elements in religious experience. Whitehead speaks of a particular providence for particular occasions.

The affirmation of God's physical pole, more often referred to as the Consequent Nature, also made it possible for Whitehead to deal with a keen existential problem. For him the passage of time and the fading of the past undercut the sense of importance or meaning. If all that we do and are is soon as if it had never been, it is finally trivial. But if God is physical as well as mental, then God shares all that we are with us. And what in the world is ephemeral is in God everlasting. Importance is restored.

VI

Whitehead's extension of his thought of God to the Consequent Nature establishes the point of contact with Hartshorne that has been so important in process theology. Hartshorne's discussion of God together with all his arguments for the existence of God relate almost exclusively to what Whitehead calls God's Consequent Nature. Hence whatever convincing power is to be found in Hartshorne's reasoning reenforces the somewhat tentative speculation of Whitehead. Schubert Ogden has supplemented this discussion with an explicit argument for belief in God, meaning here the Consequent Nature of God, from the inescapability of the sense of meaning and the inherent presupposition by it of just such a belief.

In my own writing I have concentrated attention on the mental pole of God, which Whitehead calls the Primordial Nature, and its action in the world. This reflects both the greater confidence I have felt about this reality and my judgement that it had been neglected by most process theologians. However, I have always rejoiced in the further speculations of Whitehead and the arguments and analyses of Hartshorne and Ogden. And for a variety of reasons my own enthusiasm for the full doctrine has grown. The far richer Biblical piety it supports is important to me. The exceptional experiences to which it appeals for confirmatory evidence seem real. The problem of meaning to which it responds grows more urgent. The idea of God without a physical pole seems conceptually incoherent. Also, it is through the Consequent Nature of God that process theology makes contact with feminist thinking about God or the Goddess. Finally, efforts to test Whitehead's speculations against the experience of mystics has provided further confirmation for the Consequent Nature.

At the same time that I have grown more assured of the basic vision of God, I have become even more aware of its conceptual ambiguities and limitations. Whitehead's own thought developed through his writings, and not all that he says is consistent. His intuitions often outran his concepts and analyses. Efforts to co-ordinate the insights of Hartshorne with those of Whitehead often lead to further perplexities. Almost any question about God when pressed far enough turns up new problems and uncertainties. Perhaps we have already gone too far in trying to formulate clear and coherent concepts about that which must be so different from all the creatures in relation to which our categories must first be shaped. There is confusion enough in application to the creatures!

Nevertheless, I support continued speculation when it enlarges coherence and illumines experience, whether common or extraordinary. This speculation at times also makes contact with the speculations of imaginative scientists and helps to form hypotheses for eventual testing. But that is not the present topic. What is relevant for the philosophy of religion is the co-ordination of speculation with the religious wisdom of the human race.

VII

Viewing the situation from the vantage point of Whiteheadian metaphysics, it appears that the Biblical faiths have oriented themselves to God while the deepest Indian traditions have sought to realize creativity. If so, the question of the relation of Indian to Biblical traditions is bound up with the metaphysical question of the relation of creativity and God. Hence further speculation here is far from idle.

The speculation in question already exists in the literature of both East and West. In Hinduism there is a distinction between Brahman, the Ultimate Reality, and Ishvara, the personal God. In Buddhism there is a similar distinction between Dharmakaya, the Ultimate beyond all characteristics, and Sambhogakaya, the Ultimate as wise and compassionate. In Christian mysticism Being Itself can be identified with Godhead in distinction from the personal God.

In all these cases, there is a strong tendency to subordinate God to Ultimate Reality. For example, Ultimate Reality is held to 'manifest' itself as God. The fullest, deepest religious journey carries one past the personal deity to the Ultimate that is beyond it, in Tillich's terms, to the God beyond the God of Biblical religion, that is, to Being Itself. None of this is acceptable from the point of view of Biblical faith. The predominant unwillingness of Christians to allow the distinction between God and Ultimate Reality stems in part from the impossibility of thinking of God as subordinate to something else.

Unfortunately, some of Whitehead's own language suggests this subordination. He speaks of God as a 'creature' of creativity and even as an 'accident' of creativity. Less misleading language would be that God, like every actual entity, is an instantiation of creativity, specifically, its primordial instantiation apart from which there could be no creativity. Is the instantiation subordinate to that which it instantiates? If it is, then to be actual is necessarily to be 'subordinate' to actuality-as-such, or creativity. But surely this is not a normal use of the idea of 'subordinate'.

Whitehead's best statement, in my judgement, is one in which his opposition to linear and hierarchical thinking is most clearly expressed. He writes: 'It is the function of actuality to characterize the creativity, and God is the eternal, primordial character. But, of course, there is no meaning to "creativity" apart from its "creatures", and no meaning to "God" apart from the "creativity" and the "temporal creatures", and no meaning to the "temporal creatures" apart from "creativity" and "God"'.[1] Clearly creativity, God and the temporal creatures all presuppose one another. Let us call creativity 'Ultimate Reality', God, 'Ultimate Actuality', and creatures, 'the ultimate Locus of the Actualization of Value'.

VIII

This formulation suggests three ways in which people can focus their attention and establish religious traditions. They may attend to creativity, seeking to realize Ultimate Reality by whatever name. They may place their trust in God, the giver of life and light, freedom and responsibility, order and novelty, apart from whom no creature comes into being. They may commit themselves to the attainment of value in the world, the only place where value can be achieved.

A Whiteheadian theology, then, denies the subordination of God to anything whatever, but it does not claim that God exhausts the ultimate or attempt to subordinate all else that is ultimate to God. It does not assert that all religious attention should be directed theistically. It does affirm the truth and rightness of faith in the Ultimate Actuality, while being open to learn from those who have attended more fully to Ultimate Reality and to the Ultimate Locus of the Actualization of Value. It holds that in the end each has much to learn from the other two and that in the ideal fullness of experience and understanding all would be present without subordination.

Clearly such a democracy of ultimates runs counter to the tendency in each tradition to treat the ultimate to which it has attended as *the* Ultimate. I can testify to the difficulty of persuading Buddhists that the Sambhogakaya should not be subordinated in thought or practice to the Dharmakaya! It is still more difficult to engender in committed secularists an interest in either creativity or God. And I know the deep resistance of Christians to the suggestion that there can be an ultimate not exhausted by God. Yet I believe none will sacrifice what is really central to them in such moves. The value and validity of realizing Emptiness are not reduced by the recognition that there is also value and validity in faith in God and in actualizing values in the world. The value and validity of faith in God are not reduced by the recognition that there is also value and validity in the realization of Emptiness and in actualizing values in the world. Nor is the importance of actualizing value in the world undercut by the realization of Emptiness or faith in God.

Metaphysical speculation may also help us to understand how a particular religious experience may not always be related to just one or another of these ultimates. Whitehead once wrote that in God creativity acquired a primordial character. The acquisition is, of course, primordial rather than temporal. There has never been creativity without God and there can be no experience of creativity from which God is absent. We can understand the Buddhist Sambhogakaya as the Dharmakaya as characterized by God.

Approaching from the other side we can see that there can be no experience of God apart from creativity. Attention may focus on the personal actuality of God. But it may also focus on God as that which gives a gracious character to creativity in general. Distinctions are not always sharply made in experience and language between the God who characterizes creativity and the creativity as thereby characterized.

IX

Obviously reflections of this sort are not to be found in the Bible. God is the only 'ultimate' there considered. Does that mean that what I have called 'God' cannot be the same reality to whom the Bible testifies? Some Christians take this position. They insist that the Bible testifies to an Ultimate who cannot be interdependent with other ultimates.

Such objections are, however, anachronistic. The Bible testifies to the Ultimate Actuality alongside which there are no other Ultimate Actualities. Every other actuality depends on this one for its existence and well-being. This one depends on no other actuality for its existence. So much is clear in Biblical teaching, and I affirm it also.

But the Bible does not teach that this one Ultimate is also the ultimate material cause of all things, that is, the stuff of the world. What the ultimate stuff is, is not a question raised in the Bible. If it is referred to at all it is as the chaos out of which God created. God is not the chaos! It did not occur to either Hebrews or Greeks to seek salvation through the realization of that chaos or nothingness. God may be ultimate in the lines of efficient, final, or formal causes, but not in the line of material causes.

When, then, Christians discover that some people have oriented themselves to the ultimate in the line of material causes, what do they do? One move is to extend the notion of God to include this also. Indeed, this has been the major theological move. But it has removed the God of Christian theology far from the God of the Bible, and it has introduced into Christian teaching about God incoherences that evoke incredulity. My proposal is that theology will be more faithful to the Bible and less confused in its affirmations if it recognizes that what is attested there is *not* the material cause of all things. There *is* another Ultimate in addition to God. But it is not another God alongside the Biblical one. There is one God beside whom there is no other. In that God we may place unqualified trust.

Notes

1.   Alfred North Whitehead, *Process and Reality*, corrected edition by David Ray Griffin and Donald W. Sherburne (New York: Free Press, 1978) p. 225.

6

Reply: Cobb on Ultimate Reality

Robert Merrihew Adams

I

One of Professor Cobb's aims in 'A Process Concept of God' is to find a way of seeing different religous traditions as complementary rather than competitive. This is an appealing project. How is it to be accomplished? A central point of Cobb's strategy is to assign the religious contemplation of the being of all things, including ourselves, to such traditions as Vedanta and Buddhism, as a characteristic approach quite distinct from the focus on a personal God. I have misgivings about this strategy. Perhaps Vedanta could be happy enough with it, but I suspect it does violence to other traditions.

I cannot speak with much authority on behalf of Buddhism or the mysticism of Emptiness, but I wonder whether they will be content with the assignment of 'Ultimate Reality', and the contemplation of the *being* of which all things are constituted, 'the ultimate in the line of material causes', as their special concern. Is the Emptiness of which they speak an *ontological* element of this sort? Is it to be identified with being-itself? I had thought that that was one of the things that Emptiness was not.

I would also say, and with more confidence, that in relation to personalistic theism, the religious contemplation of our own and other being as such is not unoccupied territory that can cheerfully be assigned to other religious traditions. Theists reflect on their own and other being and are convinced that what they see is the radical contingency of everything in the world, including themselves. This goes naturally with belief in a personal deity who is the ground of our being in the sense that that deity has created us out of nothing.

It is not the case, therefore, that contemplation of the deepest nature of our own being yields results that are agreed on by all but exploited by some religious traditions rather than others. On the contrary, such contemplation is experienced in some religious traditions as leading to a vision of our identity with a necessary and eternal reality, but in other traditions as leading to a vision of the vast difference between creator and creature, between independent and dependent being. Perhaps these visions are not as opposed as they seem, but at any rate the apparent conflict cannot be resolved by assigning this field of contemplation to one religious tradition, or one conception of the Ultimate, rather than another. For the field will be claimed by many traditions and many conceptions of the Ultimate.

II

I also have questions about Professor Cobb's suggestion that Ultimate Reality should be understood as the ultimate in the line of *material causes*. Some of the candidates that he discusses for the role of constituents of being fit the notion of material cause pretty well. This is true of energy and matter-energy; and, of course, the conception of material cause is built into the idea of prime matter. These are not Cobb's favourite concepts for the description of Ultimate Reality, however. He seems to prefer to speak of it as creativity, or 'creativity-itself'. He also characterizes it as 'actuality-itself', 'reality-itself', 'existence-itself', 'being-itself', and 'dynamism-itself'. None of these terms sound as if they should refer to material causes, on any historic conception of the Aristotelian 'four causes' with which I am familiar. 'Creativity' and 'dynamism' actually sound like formal or exemplar rather than material causes.

This issue has the following importance for our theological topic. Personalistic theism's account of the foundations of our being has typically included a belief in creation *ex nihilo*. This belief is one way of articulating a vision of our radical contingency and of the great qualitative difference between creator and creature. And the identification of Ultimate Reality with a material cause of our being is incompatible with creation *ex nihilo*.

The view that I exemplify (contingently and within limits) a property, *being*, or *creativity*, that is eternally and necessarily exemplified (by God) is quite consistent with the doctrine of creation *ex nihilo*. That doctrine was never intended to exclude the eternal and necessary existence of universals that we instantiate. On the other hand, the attribution of necessary or eternal existence to a *material* component of any creature is precisely what the doctrine of creation *ex nihilo* is meant to exclude. Aquinas, to take the obvious example, explicitly identifies God as the efficient, exemplar, and final cause of all things, but not as their material cause.[1]

Why has theistic tradition thus supposed that it is consistent with the difference between God and creatures to locate Ultimate Reality in other sorts of cause but not in a material cause of our being? Perhaps because it has seemed easier to see causes of other types as transcendent and distinct from us in an important way. If God's creativity is an eternal and necessary exemplar cause, our creativity can be viewed as only a copy or imitation of it, and an imperfect copy at that. But if there were an eternal and necessary material cause of creatures, they would actually be composed of it, and its existence would be completely contained in that of the sum of the things composed of it – or so I think it has been thought.

The question whether theistic tradition has made an unwarranted discrimination at this point against the material cause is worth re-examining; and Professor Cobb may wish to urge us to re-examine it. But identification of Ultimate Reality with being-itself or creativity-itself will not lead to such a re-examination unless Cobb can provide an argument, which I have not seen, for regarding those as material causes.[2]

Notes

1. Thomas Aquinas, *Summa Theologiae*, I, q. 44.
2. I am indebted to Marilyn McCord Adams for helpful discussion of previous drafts of this comment.

7

Comment on John Cobb

Stephen T. Davis

Philosophy, as we know it in the West, began in ancient Milesia. People asked the question of ultimate reality in this way: what is everything ultimately made of? Interestingly, after nearly 26 centuries of philosophy and theology, Cobb wants to ask the question in a similar way. With a slight refinement he asks: what is it that that of which all things are made (or at least all things without components) is a form? Cobb recognizes that there are other legitimate ways of asking the question of ultimate reality and other answers to the question than God. Cobb argues that his view of God possesses appropriate continuity with the use of the term in Scripture and in the Christian tradition and, in most respects, I agree.

I am dubious, however, about his denial of the claim that God is ultimate in the line of material causes. Of course the God of Christianity is not the material cause of things in the sense that the marble is the material cause of the statue. Material objects are not made of God or of God's substance. But I would argue that any denial of the notion that God is the cause of the existence of all material things, and indeed of material reality itself, is a radical departure from the tradition, not appropriately continuous with it. If material reality exists only because God created it, that is, if there would be no material reality apart from God (as in my opinion the tradition virtually unanimously affirms), then God *is* (in this sense) ultimate in the line of material causes.

8

Response to Stephen Davis

John B. Cobb, Jr.

Stephen Davis is afraid that my position diverges from the Christian tradition by failing to affirm that God is the cause of the existence of all material things. He agrees with me that this does not mean that God is the ultimate material cause. But he thinks that 'if there would be no material reality apart from God then God is ultimate in the line of material causes'.

Our dispute seems to be verbal. I agree that apart from God there could be no material thing, or any other kind of thing. God is a necessary cause of the existence of any thing whatsoever. My point is that God is not the only necessary cause of the existence of things. Things require a 'material cause' as well.

This does not mean that there exists alongside of God another being. The material cause is not a being. It does not exist in separation from the beings or things of which God is a necessary cause. I am not affirming a dualism. But the fact that a material cause is also necessary for the existence of things has not been thematized in the Christian tradition. I am consciously trying to develop and modify the tradition, but I am not breaking with it in the way Davis fears.

Part III

9

Feminism and the Christ

June O'Connor

The topic I was invited to address for this discussion was listed initially as 'The Feminist Concept of God (?)'. The question mark is well placed. As I studied this title, I became acutely conscious that it would be impossible for me to address 'The Feminist Concept of God' since I do not believe there is such a creature. Rather, there are many feminist concepts of God insofar as there are many traditions out of which feminists think and many feminists thinking about such matters.

By 'feminist' I mean generally one whose commitment to the value of gender justice and to the work its achievement requires, given the male-favoured features of our cultural heritage, leads one to become particularly attuned to women. This means awareness of the absence and the presence of women throughout the tradition, the silence and the words of women, women as agents and women as objects. It means being on the alert to ways women experience life, the viewpoints they hold, the questions they ask, the analyses and judgements they offer. The use of the plural (*women's experiences, questions, analyses,* and so forth) is deliberate. In no sense do I believe there is *a woman's point of view*. There are, rather, women's points of view, many of them. Given the masculinist bias of our patriarchal heritage, feminist scholars seek to pay attention to women whose experiences and views have been largely ignored, discounted or suppressed. Feminist scholarship thus contains an epistemological bias insofar as it seeks to disclose and discuss insights and oversights regarding women and their experience.[1] Feminist scholarship does not determine in advance where the questions will lead or what answers will be forthcoming. In this sense it is without bias: feminist scholarship is a method of inquiry, not a set of predetermined positions (Pellauer, 1985, 34).

Rosemary Ruether has stated clearly a viewpoint that I share: namely, that there is no final, definitive, universal feminist theology;

on the contrary, there are in principle many feminist theologies possible from within many religious and cultural traditions (Ruether, 1983, 20–1).

Since theology consists in reflection on experience in light of a faith tradition, one of the first tasks of the theologian is to acknowledge the experience that grounds her reflection.[2] In the words of Sallie McFague,

> Each theologian can only try to identify as clearly as possible the perspective from which she or he reflects, the tradition out of which he or she comes, and the sensibility which prompts one chosen perspective rather than another. Then, in conversation with other perspectives, the inadequacies, limitations, and possible errors can be mitigated. (McFague, 1982, viii)

In agreement with this viewpoint, Christian feminist theology seeks to be explicit about its perspectives, traditions and sensibilities. Feminist theology highlights the androcentric character of biblical texts and ecclesial-doctrinal statements which reflect and serve the patriarchal presupposition that the male is the normative human being. This feminist perspective is supported by several facts: that most of the biblical writings are ascribed to men; that the majority of theological and virtually all of the ecclesial-doctrinal writings have come to us from men; that woman has been associated with evil, sin and temptation; that women have been excluded from access to theological studies throughout most of Christian history. Since feminist theology regards androcentrism in the Christian tradition as offering a skewed vision of the human experience, it seeks to highlight the equality and full value of both female and male. It seeks also to rethink, reform and transform androcentric theology so that it becomes inclusive theology.

In addition to being explicit about its own particular perspectives, sensibilities and traditions, however, feminist theology, like other forms of theological discourse, also makes universal claims. Although it speaks out of a special sensitivity to women's experience because women's experience has largely been ignored, feminist theology seeks to clarify men's experience as well. It seeks to broaden the theological reach to an awareness of the human that is sensitive to both women's experience and analysis and to men's experience and analysis. This fuller awareness of the human as female and male prompts universal claims, that is, offers interpretations about the whole of human experience and the nature of reality as well as historical insight into this person or that event. The historical work of feminist theological research, through which lost traditions and suppressed visions are recovered, is thus complemented by systematic feminist theology.

A great deal of feminist thinking about the Christian concept of God has focused on the centrality of the imagery of God the Father.[3] Many of these feminist theological critiques have highlighted two facts: first, that the fatherhood of God is one, and only one, of the many images of God contained in the historical tradition; and second, that the Christian community needs to recover for both theology and liturgy the numerous, illuminating, and father-relativizing images that are part of this heritage. These are mother, midwife, female beloved, dame wisdom, and others (Mollencott, 1983).

Rather than rehearse the findings of this literature, I wish to consider a topic about which less has been written to date, namely, feminist christology.[4] Christology suggests a particularly problematic area for feminist theologians who by definition critique male bias, privilege and control in the tradition. The maleness of Jesus is a fact to be reckoned with, not a metaphor to be relativized. The question thus emerges: What might a feminist perspective contribute to christology?

FEMINIST CHRISTOLOGY

Feminist christology sees no ultimate theological significance in the maleness of Jesus. Because feminist theology takes seriously the full humanity and value of women, biblically-based affirmations that women and men alike are made in the image and likeness of God, are called to responsibility and salvation in Christ, and are one in Christ (as are Greeks and Jews, slaves and lords), resonate powerfully. Jesus's male identity is accepted as a feature of his person, not as a necessary condition of incarnation. Although there is no intrinsic theological significance in Jesus's maleness, there is an admittedly 'social symbolic significance' (Ruether, 1983, 137), for Jesus undercuts the predominant mode of human relating and the foundational unit of society at his time: the first century Graeco-Roman male-favoured patriarchal household (Schüssler Fiorenza, 1983).

In contrast to the prevailing modes of thought in his time, Jesus insists that doing God's will has greater claims on one's loyalty than geneological and biological bonding. He places priority on being servant rather than lord. He esteems concern for the outcast, the poor, the needy, the socially and religiously vulnerable. The power of love is more central to his ethic than the power that is expressed as control. In these ways, Jesus provides an alternative to the vision of patriarchy: a communitarian, egalitarian vision that invites the participation of all, regardless of gender, class or race. His vision challenges the *status quo* and calls those who are willing to hear and willing to change to reconceive their ways of being with one another and for one another.

Jesus expresses a certain idealism in his hopes and ways of relating. Yet he seems not to be naive about the possibility of realizing those ideals, for he was well aware of 'the principalities and powers' – a biblical metaphor for evil forces – and he engaged in vigorous exchange with them. The biblical narratives concretize these forces in a variety of provocative images: Satan, who embodies the lure of power over others, possession of things, and excessive self-confidence; intransigent religious leaders who were quite clear about how God worked and thus did not need to ask any questions; and the interior sense of foreboding that can overtake one who is feeling uncertain, fearful and alone.

The Jesus portrayed in the Christian scriptures is a man in a patriarchal society who addressed women as peers, as hearers of his word, as participants in his movement. Jesus is presented as a man who departed from the reigning mentality that regarded women as property of the household, subject to fathers and husbands, outsiders with respect to institutional religious, commercial and political affairs. This acceptance does not appear to be acquiescence. His candour with people as well as his concerns for them moved him often to challenge their biases and misconceptions. He did this with respect to their understanding of God, the place of the law, the meaning of leadership and the matter of what ultimately is important in life.

The history of christology, however, can be understood as a process by which the significance of this Jesus the Christ was gradually and increasingly moulded until it fitted in with a hierarchical, patriarchal, monarchical model. The 'patriarchalization of Christology' has been identified as part of the emergence of the institutional and imperial Christian Church. Messianic symbolism is charged with Kingship symbolism; Christ becomes the Pantocrator, the All-Ruler of a new world order. This order is cast as one of superordination and subordination: as the Logos governs the cosmos, the Christian Roman Empire and Church govern the political universe, masters govern slaves, and men govern women. The maleness of Jesus the Christ becomes viewed as an ontological necessity (Ruether, 1983, 126; 1981, 45, 48; Cooper, 1980, 192–3).

As heirs of these biblical and post-biblical historical perspectives, contemporary Christians are faced with what Gordon Kaufman names a 'deeply ambiguous christology' (1985, 52). There is, on the one hand, a portrait of a Jesus who gives himself to all sorts of persons in service and healing and invitation. And, on the other hand, there is Jesus the Christ who enjoys a privileged place with God the Father Almighty. Kaufman's response to this ambiguity is to abandon it; he urges the focus to be placed not on Jesus's nature but on human actions. Kaufman sees it as 'no longer appropriate' to engage in christological reflection 'within a framework characterized by such massive ambiguities' (1985, 53). Salvation should be the concern and should be understood, he suggests, not in the sense of an action coming down from on high and working through the church, but as the work of enhancing the quality of life for others and liberating people from the evils which enslave them (1985, 59). 'In short, wherever a spirit of creativity and liberation and healing, of reconciliation and reconstruction, is at work in the world, there is to be seen saving activity. To give ourselves over to such reconciling and healing and liberating work in human affairs is to participate in the salvific work of the divine spirit' (1985, 57).

Feminist theology, like political and liberation theology, shares this decided interest in the soteriological and ethical dimensions of christology. Feminist christology highlights the message and praxis of Jesus and views with suspicion the patriarchalization of Christ. Setting Jesus the Christ on a divine throne removes him from the human thicket of struggle and conflict in a historically grounded cluster of communities. Yet this is precisely where and how Jesus lived. The person of Jesus, the attitudes of Jesus, the deeds of Jesus – insofar as these are accessible to us through exegetical investigation and historical reconstruction – must be the starting point of a feminist liberation christology (Sobrino, 1978; Schüssler Fiorenza, 1983).

The questions to be asked in this approach are utterly basic. What sort of person was Jesus? What were his central interests, worries, loyalties, hopes and values? How did he relate to those around him?

Did gender make a difference in his responses to people and in his expectations of them? For what did he hope and for what did he die? While these questions focus attention on Jesus's message and praxis, feminist christology is less interested in the personal attributes of Jesus than in the personal and political processes in which he was involved and through which he expressed his values (Sobrino, 1978, 133).

Feminist christology highlights the fact that Jesus participated in a project far larger than himself that invites attention and participation by succeeding generations. It is a project that seeks to make real the values of spiritual sensitivity, right relations (justice), loving empathy, honesty, mercy and peace-making. The struggle to incarnate these values can be every woman's struggle and every man's struggle, whether Christian or not, religious or not. Jesus's willingness to engage in this struggle becomes a principal value for people who see and feel the need in their own time and place for the presence of these values. Feminist Christians who are keenly attuned to the need for gender justice may highlight the inequities in gender relations. But they also insist on the need for targeting the numerous injustices that pervade modern life: classism, racism, militarism, religious, economic, political and species exclusivism. A feminist christology that places initial attention on the message and praxis of Jesus seeks to glean from that message and praxis insights that are transferable to current life struggles. Attention is placed on his praxis rather than on the nature of his person.

Yet attention to process does not and cannot displace attention to person. The tradition's manifest interest in the person and nature of Jesus cannot be suspended on the grounds that its massive ambiguities can no longer be accepted as appropriate. Concern with Jesus's praxis necessarily includes concern with his person, both because of the need to unmask ways in which christology has been used against women and because responsible faith requires a long hard look at the one accepted in faith. Over the centuries the Christian community has studied the person of Jesus. The conviction that Jesus is the one in whom human beings are given access to God, a foundational theme in Christian thought present even before the New Testament texts were put together, developed into a creedal and doctrinal affirmation that Jesus is God as well as man. How might a Christian feminist theology deal with the claim that Jesus is God, that Jesus embodies God, incarnates God, expresses God in a distinctive and unique fashion?

A FEMINIST CLASSICAL CHRISTOLOGY?

Feminist christology, like many contemporary theologies, assumes that one must abandon in advance the search for certainty. It regards the question itself as inherently valuable, worthy of pursuit, and one to be lived with. Is it so? Has God truly entered human experience in a distinctive way in Jesus? No, the synoptics suggest. Yes, the fourth gospel proudly proclaims. Yes, a conciliar chorus rings forth (Nicea, Chalcedon), offering its explanation in Greek philosophical categories. No, a theological chorus resounds (Hick, 1977), offering its reasons in categories influenced by modern psychology.

Given this variety of conflicting arguments and claims within the tradition itself, the Christian wonders which to accept. Are the earlier gospels the more authentic ones, the later gospels the more embellished and therefore less trustworthy, as current critical biblical scholarship concludes? Or could it be that the earlier, synoptic portraits of Jesus are the unfinished and incomplete rough draft, those first sketch preliminaries that precede the finished portrait? Do these synoptic impressions, perhaps, season with time and become more aptly and more accurately cast by the fourth evangelist after matured meditation, reflection and realization?

These questions not only suggest differing answers; they suggest different orientations in reflection and differing sensibilities about the sources of one's trust. Although feminist christology rejects the patriarchalization of Christ because that mode of thought casts Jesus as a hierarchically envisaged authority that fosters distance and domination and is at odds with the egalitarian ethic presented in his words and deeds, feminist christology does not necessarily reject the unique divinity of Jesus. Feminist theologians address that question according to a variety of models expressing what is meant by the unity of divinity and humanity in Jesus and how that might be understood.

One line of thought seeks to de-divinize Jesus because claims about Jesus being a divine saviour alienate women from themselves. Rita Brock, for example, voices the position that women must reclaim themselves as the source of their own salvation, that is, of their own healing and growth into wholeness. Having reclaimed themselves as source of their own power and hope, they are then in a position 'to reclaim the historical Jesus and Jesus Christ'. To do this is to 'reclaim Jesus as a remarkable man for his time' and to reclaim ('redeem') Christ by participating in a new way in Christ, that is, in 'the community remembrance of the Jesus who lived on earth' which is what she means by Christ (Brock, 1984, 68–71). Carter Heyward regards Jesus as fully human and only human. Claims about Jesus's divinity are equated with claims about a distant, pre-existent, alien and alienating patriarchal God. To affirm Jesus's divinity is for Heyward to remove him from human experience and to deny the Christian's responsibility to make God incarnate (Heyward, 1981, 33–4).

Another line of thinking, also stimulated by the feminist concern to de-patriarchalize theology, nonetheless articulates a christology that affirms both divinity and humanity in Jesus Christ. Bernard Cooke, Geoffrey Lilburne and Burton Cooper share the feminist critical perspective on patriarchy, disclosing and denouncing imagery of domination, subordination and male superiority. Each affirms the uniqueness of Jesus's relationship to God and struggles to articulate that relationship in a way that coherently affirms both divinity and humanity. Each finds relational categories fundamental. Cooke discusses the 'intimacy' of the relationship that Jesus experienced with God; he describes this experience as one of 'immediacy' and finds Jesus's use of the expression 'Abba' to suggest a wholly new content to the term Father. God-the-father was understood by the Hebrews as a metaphor for a transcendent God and should be so understood by us, he asserts. But God-the-Father-of-Jesus indicates an experience of God unique to Jesus that suggests to Cooke something qualitatively different from other human relationships with God (Cooke, 1983).

Lilburne finds in Jesus's relation to God 'the intersection of two personal patterns of intentional-action'. He suggests that the feminist christology articulated by Rosemary Ruether (1981) offers intriguing avenues for reaffirming Jesus's divinity as well as humanity. For in Ruether's soteriology, if not explicitly in her christology, one finds affirmations of 'intersections between the intentionality of Jesus and the purposes of God, between the acts of Jesus and the saving activity of God' (Lilburne, 1984, 14).

Cooper finds a Whiteheadian metaphysics more congenial to an adequate restatement of christology. Whitehead's model of causation alerts us to the internal reception or 'prehension' of causal factors rather than limiting us to a model that relies on external actions and interactions where behavioural actions may change but the internal make-up of the being or 'occasion' does not. Thus God's way of acting upon and receiving the world is prehensively, through internal appropriation, not by externally moving things into relationship. The relation of the divine to the human in Jesus can now be thought of not in terms of an external union of two inseparable natures but of a mutual internal appropriating communion of feelings. 'In Jesus, we can affirm a life which so intensely, even uniquely, feels the being, love, and suffering of God as to elicit from him a response conforming his will and being to God's will and being.' For Cooper, in contrast to Cooke, Jesus's relationship to God is not qualitatively different, but differs only in 'intensity, intent, and historical relevance'. Thus 'Jesus' unique and divine significance. . . . lies in his being the chief exemplification and full embodiment of God's incarnate power of love for the world' (Cooper, 1980, 188–9).

The adequacy of these as of any theological efforts must be examined in relation to two reference points: (1) the tradition as this has been expressed biblically, theologically and ecclesially (which includes ethics, doctrine and liturgy); and (2) the plausibility test, that is, whether it seems possible, likely, realistic, in light of human experience and knowledge.

TRADITION

The claim that there is a unique and unrepeatable identity between Jesus and God does seem integral to the tradition in a way its negation does not. Son of God, pre-existent Logos, oneness with the Father, consubstantiality with the Father and with humanity, and union of two distinct natures in one person illustrate some of the phrases which have been formative in the past and with which contemporary reconceptualizations must reckon.

In itself, the argument from tradition is not a compelling one for feminist theology which employs a hermeneutics of suspicion when examining historical materials. Mary Daly's dictum that 'if God is male, then the male is God'[5] illuminates the feminist interest in a hermeneutics of suspicion. It is undeniable that christology has been used and continues to be used to enhance and protect male privilege and to dismiss, reject and exclude women. But christology can function otherwise. For while christological claims have been used to favour patriarchal privilege, a feminist, post-patriarchal theological consciousness can expose this usage and work to recover a deeper awareness of who Christ is and what God is like. What is uncovered, recovered and discovered is a God who affirms the value of embodiment by being embodied and who fosters mutuality rather than hierarchy, interdependent differentiation rather than domination and subordination, and freedom as empowerment in contrast to freedom as control.

PLAUSIBILITY

The plausibility argument, I propose, is stronger than the argument from tradition and can be developed in at least two ways. First, the feminist interest in and concern with concrete, bodily being leads feminist theologians to examine a classical christology with decided interest. The very idea of an integral divine/human, spirit/flesh union is inherently attractive, as the basic human experiences of love suggest. For when we want to show another that we love her or him, what do we do? We extend ourselves to be near the other, seeking to become one in heart, mind, will, perhaps even body. What is he feeling, we wonder, what are her interests, concerns, worries and aspirations? What can we do to enhance that person's experience? How enable and empower him to live rightly? Answers to these questions come with the sharing of time and place, with mutual expression and communication. As the spirituality tradition has long insisted, to love God, likewise, is to seek union with God, to identify heart, mind and will with God insofar as that is possible to finite human experience. So, too, if indeed God intended/intends to show love to the human community, what better way is there for God to do so than to be with the human community in a way that enables God to identify with people, understand them from within their own experience (empathy *par excellence*), and know in a deeply felt manner what human being feels like? The strategy of identification with human experience, with all the particularity and limitation that form of existence brings with it, makes sense, seems to be a good and wise way to be, given the psychology and the value of love.

To the extent that Jesus symbolizes the divine affirmation of bodiliness as a way of being, he provides an embodiment model for human spirituality. If Jesus gives the human community a glimpse into what God is like, God becomes understood as a loving and challenging friend who is at home with physical, material, bodily being. This resonates powerfully with the feminist affirmation of the concreteness of women's experience (as of men's) informing universalized generalizations about human life and thus rendering these generalizations more accurately than those rooted in male experience alone.

Second, such an expression of God ('as' Jesus, 'in' Jesus, 'with' Jesus) can be viewed as a powerful way of making the Christian point. What seems particularly notable about a Jesus-is-divine-as-well-as-human story is that in such a case God would be doing what God is saying. Word and action would be one. God loves human beings, the story unfolds, and they are invited to love as God loves, by way of identification, empathy and personal presence, in grace and struggle alike. Given such a message, a scenario of events in which God becomes embodied (or, as some would prefer, a human person divinized) could be/would be (one might conjecture in advance) a wonderfully clear, powerful and effective way to make a point. Pedagogically considered, it can be judged an impressive, imaginative, brilliant idea.

The question, however, nags: did it happen? is it true? no matter how beautiful, is it so? If, as Keats's poetry and Aquinas's metaphysics suggest, beauty and truth are one, one wonders if the truthfulness of the claim might be found precisely here, in its beauty. It is, as a story, beautiful to many. Nonetheless, the modern asks insistently, is it true ontologically? Or is it 'only' true aesthetically?

This either/or formulation of the concern reminds one of the provocative position of an Oglala Sioux holy man who recounts being faced with a similar question. Reflecting on the accuracy of an historical claim about one of his religio-cultural myths,[6] Black Elk concluded, 'This they tell, and whether it happened so or not I do not know; but if you think about it, you can see that it is true'.[7] Might we not adapt the wisdom of his remark and say of the Jesus-is-God-as-well-as-human story: 'This they tell, and whether it happened so or not I do not know; but if you think about it, you can see that it is true'? The beauty of the story carries a truth of its own. Perhaps an aesthetic understanding of truth would serve theology better than a model of truth as verifiable. Yet to theologians nurtured by a sense of history with an appreciation of ontology, such an aesthetic christology could never satisfy. Given the classic triad of the True, the Good and the Beautiful, the theologian is haunted by the True. For theologians who value historical critical exegesis, interpretation, recovery, and reconstruction, the Beautiful cannot, in the end, be trusted. Beauty can delude and seduce as well as impress and inspire.

A FEMINIST FANTASY

To think about the incarnational myth of the Christian inheritance invites conjecture and even fantasy about other ways the point could have been made, other ways the myth might have been cast, other ways the story might have unfolded. A feminist christology finds it attractive to envision a human God as twins, one female and one male. This feminist theologian fully recognizes the culture-specific and generation-specific stance from which such a fantasy emerges – from the standpoint of attunement to the need for models of gender equality. Its appeal is rooted in the fact that such a male and female embodiment might have prevented the male mystification known as patriarchy. Yet this fantasy is offered with self-critical awareness that other modes of identification might have prevented other evils. (Why did God not make Jesus's identity unambiguous and thus the patristic period's theological battles unnecessary? Why did God not set us straight about 'error's rights' and prevent the Inquisition?)

The fantasy is also offered in self-critical consciousness that history precludes the possibility of complete identification. Jesus is a first-century Jewish carpenter's son from Galilee. Thus he is temporally, geographically, ethnically, occupationally, educationally and sexually different from generations of sympathizers and followers. Gender is one and only one of many many differences. Feminist reflection requires that just as we have not absolutized the temporal, geographical, ethnic or occupational identity of Jesus, so we should not absolutize his male identity either.

CONCLUSION

These reflections on the plausibility of the classical theological claim that Jesus experienced a unique relationship with God, so much so that it makes sense and is accurate to describe Jesus as both divine and human, articulate one way in which feminist christology might recover what genuine insights lie behind the conviction that Jesus is one of the human community and God. Taking such a claim seriously then requires that attention be placed on Jesus's existence in order to gain an understanding of what God is like. The God discovered, feminists note, is not the patriarch often presented.

The plausibility claim addressed here joins the conversation, does not close the conversation. Other nagging questions – such as how more precisely such an affirmation about Jesus can be understood and how we might understand the tradition's claims to exclusivity, especially in light of the pluralism of religions – also require fresh attention. The plausibility claim highlighted here is simply one feminist critical response to the view that an incarnational christology is rooted in the group psychology of exaggerating the importance of an impressive person or rooted in an idolatrous proclivity to worshipping the visible. The plausibility claim explored here offers alternative grounds: the dynamics of giving love and artful pedagogy.

A question persists: can one be certain that one discovers God in Jesus? The problem this question raises is no different from the problem of theology in general. Awareness of the perspectival character of knowledge, the complex dynamics of human psychology, and the very nature of religious reality as transcendent to as well as immanent within sensible, historical reality preclude the possibility of certitude. Certitude is not a theological option. What is available is a process of reflection responsive to experience, history and critical analysis through which we ponderously gain insight and struggle to diminish oversight. The claim of this chapter is that a feminist christology can support, even while it seeks to transform, the fundamental affirmations of a classical incarnational christology. It cannot, just as other theologies cannot, offer certitudes that dispel doubt.

When doing theology I think it is useful to remember that religious experience generates theology, is not exhausted by theology. And experience – a vast reservoir that includes reason, emotion, volition, imagination, memory, community – occurs differently from person to person according to disposition, tradition, sensibility. The True, the Good and the Beautiful serve theological attraction variously: for some, the Jesus story engages by a ring of truthfulness that is compelling, for others it is the goodness of the story that engages them to act, still others are drawn to the beauty it portrays. Each begins somewhere, yet one access point often opens to another, alerts one to the other, connects with the other, relativizes the other. The arresting power of the Jesus story may compel one to meditate on its meaning and message; the goodness portrayed may evoke commitment and loyalty, prompting the believer to wonder about its truthfulness and to explore the question at length. Wondering if it is 'really true' (and acknowledging the hopelessness of finding scientific-type certitude to such a query) may move one to linger over the beauty of the symbol, allowing receptivity to the truth it expresses and the goodness it exemplifies.

Such a process provides the possibility of valued insight, yet presumes the impossibility of certitude. Though we long to know with certitude precisely when we are discovering what is so (independent of our viewpoints) and at what points are creating and constructing the affirmations that are voiced, we are, finally, compelled to recognize that ultimately we cannot know even that. Through a variety of intellectual disciplines (the sciences, the humanities, the arts) we gain glimpses, construct theories, formulate theologies, articulate doctrines and reconstruct history. In the final analysis we live in trust. Theology, in large measure, is a matter of reflecting critically about one's trust. Where do we place it? Why? On what grounds? For what reasons? To what ends? Efforts to answer these questions keep the theological enterprise alive, for it is by dealing with these questions that we disclose those perspectives, traditions and sensibilities which McFague rightly notes are at the heart of theological reflection. Then, in conversation with one another, 'the inadequacies, limitations, and possible errors can be mitigated' (McFague, 1982, viii). These reflections on feminist christology are offered to inform and stimulate that conversation.

Notes

1. See Caroline Walker Bynum's impressive historical study *Jesus as Mother* (1982) as one example, Jane Schaberg's fascinating exegesis in *The Illegitimacy of Jesus* (1987) as another. See particularly the writings of Rosemary Ruether (1974, 1979, 1981, 1983).
2. By reflection I include the processes of inquiry, examination, analysis, criticism, imaginative construction and reconstruction. On the latter two (imaginative construction and imaginative reconstruction), see Gordon Kaufman (1985) and Elisabeth Schüssler Fiorenza (1983).
3. See for example Mary Daly (1973), Naomi Goldenberg (1979), Phyllis Trible (1978), Sallie McFague (1982), Virginia Ramey Mollencott (1983), Rosemary Ruether (1981, 1983), Carol Ochs (1977), Elizabeth Johnson (1984), John Cobb (1983).
4. See Ruether (1981; 1983, ch. 5), Rita Brock (1984), Bernard Cooke

(1983), John Cobb (1983, 85–9), Patricia Wilson-Kastner (1983), Geoffrey Lilburne (1984), Burton Cooper (1980), and Jane Kopas (1986).
5. Mary Daly (1973, 19).
6. Myth, a highly elastic word, requires definition by anyone who uses it. By myth I mean a narrative that explains – whether it be about a person, an event, a mentality, a value system, an object or an institution. In addition to explaining, myths function to proclaim attitudes and values and to prompt questions, stimulating us to wonder, to reflect, to probe more deeply. Myth is a descriptive word meaning the word expressed, the tale told, and in itself says nothing about its truthfulness or falsity. Whether a given myth is true or false is a question that ought to be faced. But the answer is not given in the term.
7. Neihardt (1973, p. 4).

Bibliography

Brock, Rita (1984), 'The Feminist Redemption of Christ', in *Christian Feminism: Visions of a New Humanity*, ed. by Judith L. Weidman (Harper & Row) pp. 55–74.

Bynum, Caroline Walker (1982), *Jesus as Mother: Studies in the Spirituality of the High Middle Ages* (University of California).

Carr, Anne (1982), 'Is a Christian Feminist Theology Possible?', *Theological Studies*, 43/2 (June) pp. 279–97.

Cobb, John B., Jr. (1975), *Christ in a Pluralistic Age* (Westminster).

Cobb, John B., Jr. (1983), 'God and Feminism', in *Talking About God* (with David Tracy). (Seabury) pp. 75–91.

Cooke, Bernard (1983), 'Nonpatriarchal Salvation', *Horizons, Journal of the College Theology Society*, 10/1 (spring) pp. 22–31.

Cooper, Burton (1980), 'Metaphysics, Christology, and Sexism: An Essay in Philosophical Theology', *Religious Studies*, 16 (June) pp. 179–93.

Cupitt, Don (1979), *The Debate About Christ* (SCM).

Daly, Mary (1973), *Beyond God the Father* (Beacon).

Goldenberg, Naomi (1979), *The Changing of the Gods: Feminism and the End of Traditional Religions* (Beacon).

Goulder, Michael (ed.) (1979), *Incarnation and Myth: The Debate Continued* (SCM).

Harvey, A. E. (ed.) (1981), *God Incarnate: Story and Belief* (SPCK).

Heyward, Carter (1981), *The Redemption of God: A Theology of Mutual Relation* (University Microfilms).

Hick, John (ed.) (1977), *The Myth of God Incarnate* (SCM).

Hick, John (1983), *Christians and Religious Pluralism* (SCM).

Johnson, Elizabeth (1984), 'The Incomprehensibility of God and the Image of God Male and Female', *Theological Studies* 45 (summer) pp. 441–65.

Kaufman, Gordon (1985), *Theology for a Nuclear Age* (Westminster).

Kopas, Jane (1986), 'Teaching Christology in Light of Feminist Issues', *Horizons, Journal of the College Theology Society*, 13/2 (autumn) pp. 332–43.

Lilburne, Geoffrey (1984), 'Christology: In Dialogue with Feminism', *Horizons, Journal of the College Theology Society*, 11/1 (spring) pp. 7–27.

McFague, Sallie (1982), *Metaphorical Theology: Models of God in Religious Language* (Fortress).

Mollencott, Virginia Ramey (1983), *The Divine Feminine: The Biblical Imagery of God as Female* (Crossroad).

Moltmann-Wendell, Elisabeth (1982), *The Women Around Jesus* (Crossroad).

Neihardt, John (1973), *Black Elk Speaks* (Pocket).

Ochs, Carol (1977), *Behind the Sex of God: Toward a New Consciousness Transcending Matriarchy and Patriarchy* (Beacon).

Pelikan, Jaroslav (1985), *Jesus Through the Centuries: His Place in the History of Culture* (Yale).

Pellauer, Mary (1985), 'Moral Callousness and Moral Sensitivity: Violence Against Women', in Barbara H. Andolsen, Christine E. Gudorf, and Mary D. Pellauer (eds), *Women's Consciousness, Women's Conscience: A Reader in Feminist Ethics* (Seabury/Winston).

Ruether, Rosemary (1974), *Religion and Sexism* (Simon & Schuster).

Ruether, Rosemary (1979), *Women of Spirit: Female Leadership in the Jewish and Christian Traditions* (ed. with Eleanor McLaughlin) (Simon & Schuster).

Ruether, Rosemary (1981), *To Change the World: Christology and Cultural Criticism* (Crossroad).

Ruether, Rosemary (1983), *Sexism and God-Talk: Toward a Feminist Theology* (Beacon).

Schaberg, Jane (1987), *The Illegitimacy of Jesus: A Feminist Theological Interpretation of the Infancy Narratives* (Harper & Row).

Schüssler Fiorenza, Elisabeth (1983), *In Memory of Her: A Feminist Theological Reconstruction of Christian Origins* (Crossroad).

Schüssler Fiorenza, Elisabeth (1984), *Bread Not Stone: The Challenge of Feminist Biblical Interpretation* (Beacon).

Sobrino, Jon, S. J. (1978), *Christology at the Crossroads: A Latin American Approach*. Translated by John Drury (Orbis).

Suchocki, Marjorie Hewitt (1982), *God Christ Church: A Practical Guide to Process Theology* (Crossroad).

Trible, Phyllis (1978), *God and the Rhetoric of Sexuality* (Fortress).

Turner, Pauline and Bernard Cooke (1984), 'Feminist Thought and Systematic Theology', *Horizons, Journal of the College Theology Society*, 11/1 (spring) pp. 125–35.

Wilson-Kastner, Patricia (1983), *Faith, Feminism, and the Christ* (Fortress).

10

Response to
June O'Connor

Karen Torjesen

June O'Connor's chapter begins, like most discussions of feminist theology, with an elucidation of the epistemological starting point for feminist theology – which is women's experience. Here June O'Connor makes some valuable qualifications. Rather than speak of women's experience (singular), she wishes to speak of women's experiences (plural). She elaborates women's experiences in terms of viewpoints, questions, analyses and judgements (all plural); as there is a diversity of viewpoints, so there is a diversity of feminist theologies.

These are valuable qualifications, and despite their self-evidence they need to be asserted. Room must be created for all who wish to undertake feminist theology. However, I am concerned that these qualifications be kept distinct from the way in which feminist theology is applied, for the nature of theological discourse is that it makes universal claims. It reaches for a level of abstraction that can define the fundamental structure of reality and/or human experience.

In fact, it is in just this way that theology as an enterprise carried out by men only has been oppressive to women. Rationality (long identified with male nature) as a way of controlling the world places man at the centre of the cosmos which he himself orders. The impact on women is that they live in a reality defined by males and are ordered into a system described by males.

Feminism has an important function in identifying the relativity and perspectival character of all theological systems and especially the androcentric nature of the entire theological tradition. However, I am concerned that feminist theology – with full consciousness of the perspectival character of *all* theological systems – should not fail to make its own claim to universality, to interpret the whole of human experience and to make its own definition of the nature of reality. I think there are two senses in which feminist theology can lay claim to this universality. It can claim universality when it speaks to and out of and into women's experience (and here I mean women in the collective sense) and when, because it illuminates women's experience, it is also addressing and clarifying men's experience.

Let me give an example. We can speak both of women's experiences (plural) and of women's experience (singular). For while women's experiences may vary according to the cultures and traditions which shape their lives, there are also universal dimensions to women's experience that do not vary according to culture and tradition. These are the distinction between public and private spheres, the relegation of women to the private sphere, the subordination of the private to the public, and the consequent subordination of female to male. In most cultures women, because of their child-bearing functions, are defined by their domestic activities; their lives are focused on the 'particularistic' concerns of children and home. Men, on the other hand, occupy themselves with the formation of the overarching 'universalistic' structures which link particular domestic groups, and they are defined by their roles in the public sphere. Thus, women are associated with the private, men with the public sphere.

Women's experience in this sense provides an epistemological starting point that would allow a feminist theology to make a universal claim in both senses. A feminist theology with such a starting point would illuminate a universal aspect of women's experience (that is, the experience of being *untergeordnet* with respect to man and the experience of being defined in terms of her function in the private sphere). Such a feminist theology would also correspondingly interpret and define men's experience by seeing men not only as they have sought *to define* women but also as they have been *defined by* women. Thus, such a feminist theology would have not only the corrective value of incorporating 'lost traditions and suppressed visions' but would construct a system of its own – an inclusive one – into which female and male are ordered. Thus, while I am sympathetic with the need to insist that there are many feminist theologies, I would also like to maintain that it is the right and obligation of feminist theology to make universal claims.

Now I would like to turn to the intriguing and well formulated thesis of O'Connor's chapter that a feminist concept of God might be drawn from the praxis of Jesus if a unique and unrepeatable identity between Jesus and God could be asserted, that is, if – to use the language of the tradition – Jesus were divine and had the same nature as God. The immediate problem of such a thesis is that Jesus was a male. The author does not attempt to mitigate the problem, but engages it head-on. First she asks what the maleness of Jesus meant and did not mean in the first century context of Hellenistic Judaism. She finds that the maleness of Jesus does not support a patriarchal form of social organization. Both Jesus's message and praxis undercut the legitimacy of the patriarchy. Further, the maleness of Jesus does not support the attitudes of patriarchal society toward women. The message and praxis of Jesus recognized women as peers and as participators in the work of the Kingdom.

The message and praxis of Jesus have provided the basis for feminist formulations of soteriology and ethics. In these areas the maleness of Jesus has not been problematic for feminist theology. However, June O'Connor is interested in moving from christology to a feminist concept of God and so is concerned with the person of Jesus. Thus, the fact that the person of Jesus has become a supporting figure for a 'hierarchical, patriarchal, monarchical concept of God' is an obstacle to be overcome. The author refers to the process by which the Jesus of the New Testament writings became a monarchical figure as the 'patriarchalization of christology' in which 'Messianic symbolism is charged with Kingship symbolism'.

It may be helpful here to note that this process took four centuries to complete and that it first took place on the level of church organization. Not until the middle of the third century does a distinction between rulers and people, between clergy and laity (*laos* = greek for the people) emerge. The bishop who had been seen as leader of the household or household manager increasingly is seen in the role of quasi-imperial ruler. The bishop's throne, the bishop's court and the hierarchalization of the clergy are all part of this transition which led to a monarchical view of God (*ho despotes, ho pantocrator* = Greek imperial titles applied to God) and a hierarchical ordering of the trinitarian relationships with Christ subordinate to God and the Holy Spirit to Christ, and with the clergy hierarchically ordered following directly after the Holy Spirit. By the late fourth century the monarchical representations of Christ appear. This makes the christology of the first three centuries potentially interesting to feminists.

Thus the way is cleared to state the main thesis. A christology that focuses on the person as well as on the praxis of Jesus is desirable, because the praxis of Jesus reveals his person, and it is free of patriarchal values and norms and challenges the patriarchal social structure. Given a unique identity between Jesus and God, the nature of God is then defined by the praxis of Jesus, and a feminist concept of God can be articulated, namely a concept of God that can be expressed in terms of 'embodiment, mutuality, interdependent differentiation, equality, freedom as empowerment, healing and reconciliation'.

The author argues that if there were an incarnation (God taking on humanity), then incarnation as the most fundamental form of God's self-expression would yield a feminist concept of God. The project the author proposes is promising; the positing of a unique identity between Jesus and God would yield a feminist concept of God. The incarnation understood from the side of God taking on humanity would yield a feminist concept of God. There is only one problem and that is that the incarnation understood from the side of humanity (the divinization of a human person as the author formulates it) means the divinization of a male person and consequently of the male. The author's myth of an incarnation in the form of twins imaginatively illustrates the problem.

This problem is not insoluble. However, if such a feminist christology were attempted, it would have to work with a high christology, for that is the only way to avoid divinizing the male. The two natures/one person christological formulas require that the individuality (the one person-ness) be identified with the divinity rather than the humanity. Thus in the incarnation the second person of the trinity assumes the common humanity (of female and male) rather than a male person. (If the second person of the Trinity assumed a male person, then there would be two natures and two persons.) One might say that in the incarnation God in Christ took on androgynous humanity (the humanity common to both female and male). This would respond to the problem suggested in the author's notion of incarnation as twins (male and female) in that the humanity of Christ could then be understood as encompassing and expressing male and female. One might be tempted to speak of the androgynous Christ.

However, there are problems created by this solution. If the humanity of Christ can no longer be understood as the humanity of a male individual, in what sense can it be called humanity at all? This is perhaps the most valuable question of all. For what it means is that the nature of our humanity itself needs to be rethought; that is, the nature of femaleness and maleness and the way in which individuality or personhood is constituted by these. We might be led to an androgynous view of humanity of the Jungian sort, or we might be led elsewhere. Either way, the project of understanding the person of Jesus in terms of his praxis and then positing a unique identity between Jesus and God will, I believe, lead to a feminist concept of God. However, the positing of such a unique identity between Jesus and God will demand that we rethink the humanity of Jesus and in process rethink how we understand our own.

Part IV

11

The Vedic-Upanisadic Concept of Brahman (The Highest God)

Sushanta Sen

INTRODUCTORY REMARKS

In India, unlike the West, the line of demarcation between philosophy and religion is so very thin that the one often flows into the other, making her philosophy as much religious as her religion philosophical. This is particularly true of Hinduism and is evident from the fact that the Vedas, the foundational scriptures of the Hindu religion, stand as the unquestionable authority for all the six orthodox systems of Hindu philosophy (*āstika darsana*). In these systems the Vedas are often invoked as the final court of appeal in matters of philosophical controversy, or a well reasoned conclusion arrived at by a valid logical argument is sought to be corroborated by some textual citations from the Vedas as a plea for its acceptance. Indeed, the very definition of Hindu orthodoxy (*āstikya*) which distinguishes it from other non-Hindu heterodox (*ñastika*) systems of Indian religions, like Buddhism and Jainism, affirms its unqualified faith in the truth of the Vedas. This is borne out by the fact that though Hinduism in the course of time branched off into a bewildering variety of conflicting sects, none of them quarrels over the authority of the Vedas; and the Vedas are claimed to command such infallible authority because their contents are believed to be the records of direct revelation of Truth received by the pure-hearted saints and seers of remote antiquity. This persistent allegiance to the essential teachings of the Vedas explains why Hinduism is justifiably called *vaidika dharma* or the religion of the Vedas. Hence the Hindu concept of God primarily means the Vedic concept of God.

THE VEDIC-UPANISADIC TEACHINGS ON GOD: THE IDEA OF SELF-GOD (ATMAN-BRAHMAN) IDENTITY

But it is not a very easy task to distill the essence of the Vedic teachings on God out of their huge bulk and their rich diversity of metaphors and allegories. The thematic division of the Vedas into three different parts – the Samhitās, Brāhmanas and the Upanisads[1] – makes the matter more difficult, because the theme of the one part seems to contradict the theme of the other. Thus, to a casual reader cursorily glancing over the pages of the Vedas, the polytheistic overtone of the Samhitās and the Brāhmanas in admitting a number of gods (*devas*) and offering sacrificial oblation to them appears to be flatly incongruous with the strictly monotheistic conception of God that permeates the whole corpus of the Upanisadic literature. The countless passages of the Upanisads seek to elaborate one fundamental theme in a variety of ways: 'There is but one Being, not a second' (*Ekam eva advitiyam*).[2] This one universal Being has been variously termed in the Upanisads as *Brahman, Isvara, Paramātman*, and so on, for all of which the blanket English term 'God' may be used, though each one of them has a characteristic shade of meaning distinct from the others. Now, this sort of thematic discrepancy of the one part of the Vedas with the others makes it rather difficult to ascertain which one of these two parts is to be accepted as truly representing the Vedic idea of God – the polytheism of the Samhitās and the Brāhmanas or the monotheism of the Upanisads. This is a problem which we shall discuss in detail in the next section. But for the present purpose let us see if the Samhitā portion of the Vedas, where polytheism is most prominently displayed, can suggest any intelligible hint toward its solution.

We have it on the authority of the Vedas themselves as well as on the evidence of other Sanskrit writings that the 'Gāyatri' verse of the Vedas,[3] through the impartation of which a Hindu of the upper three castes is initiated for the first time into spiritual life, contains the quintessence of the entire mass of Vedic literature. In the *Atharva-Veda*, the Gāyatri has been described as the 'mother of the Vedas' (Veda-mātā)[4] containing their essential spirit. This particular cryptic verse of the Rg-Veda, therefore, should be taken as the main trunk of the great Vedic tree of which the other elements are its dispensible ramifications. In this Gāyatri verse it has been said that there is one Universal Being who is self-luminous and manifests himself in this and many other worlds; and this Being dwells in our heart as our Inner Ruler. It has been translated into English as follows:

> We meditate on the most resplendent and adorable light of the self-luminous Spirit who dwells in the heart as its inner ruler and manifests Himself as the earth, and sky and the heavens; may He guide our thoughts along the right path.[5]

This Gāyatri conception of a self-luminous Universal Spirit and of His residence in the human heart was later crystallized in the Upanisads, the concluding part of the Vedas, into the doctrine of an all-pervading *Brāhman* (God) and His identity with the individual Self (*Ātman*). The individual self, however limited and imperfect it may appear, is in its final depths Divine in nature, because 'the most resplendent and adorable light of the self-luminous spirit' dwells in it. This doctrine of the essential identity of the self (*Ātman*) with God (*Brāhman*) – first suggested in the Gāyatri verse but fully developed in the Upanisads – is, therefore, the central creed of the Vedas, and indeed of Hinduism in general. The four 'great sayings' (mahāvākyas) of the Upanisads, like 'that thou art' (*tat tvam asi*),[6] I am Brahman (*aham Brahmāsmi*), and so on, as well as countless other passages, point to this central doctrine. Since the Self and God are ultimately identical, enquiry into the nature of God resolves itself into an enquiry into the nature of the Self. This explains why the concept of *Ātman* or the Self is the pivot around which all the doctrines of the Upanisads revolve. 'What is that, Venerable Sir, which being known everything else is known?' – an eager seeker asked Angirā, the great sage of the Upanisadic period.[7] The Upanisads found the answer to this question in the knowledge of the true nature of the Self.

The Self (*Ātman*) is, according to the Upanisads, the inner essence of humanity – a permanent substance which remains fixed and constant amidst all sorts of change of the body, sense-organs and the mind. The body of a person may change beyond recognition, the sense-organs may be mutilated and the mind may be (and in fact is) in a state of incessant flux – its sensations, emotions, ideas, images and such like, are continuously gliding away one after another. But the fact that one never loses one's self-identity to oneself proves that somewhere within this ceaseless phantasmagoria there exists an abiding reality which simply witnesses these changes but does not become affected by them. This permanent immutable substance in humanity is called the *Ātman* or Self. This *Ātman*, however, is thought to be not only the *inner essence* of humanity but also the outer essence of the Universe. The Upanisads do not make any distinction between within and without. We read in the *Kathopanisad*: 'What is within us is also without. What is without is also within. He who sees difference between what is within and what is without goes evermore from death to death'.[8] When viewed as the ultimate metaphysical principle of the outer Universe, the *Ātman* is termed *Brahman*. There is endless change without in the shape of movement, growth, decay and death, and at the heart of these changes there is an abiding reality called *Brahman*. Again, at the heart of endless changes within our body-mind complex there is an abiding reality called *Ātman*, and these two principles are treated as one and the same. *Ayam Ātmā Brahman* – 'this Self is the Brahman' – is one of the 'great sayings' (*mahāvākyas*) in which the Upanisads sum up this teaching.

But a crucial question can be raised here: if an immutable changeless *Ātman* is the sole reality of humanity and the Universe, then how are we to view the phenomena of change and becoming which characterize the world of our everyday experience? The reply of Upanisadic Hinduism to this question would be that whatever undergoes change and is unstable, fleeting and evanescent cannot have any intrinsic value and reality of its own. Hence, change or becoming is to be regarded as more or less unreal and as the source of all pain and suffering of our life. It is the *Ātman* only that lies beyond any possibility of change and suffering. But though itself devoid of any suffering and change, the *Ātman*, under the spell of a cosmic nescience (*avidyā*), forgets its real nature and wrongly identifies itself with the changing phenomena of its body and mind. These latter are not parts of the Self itself but are its *Kosas*, or the sheaths within which it is wrapped. This mistaken identification of the *Ātman* with what it is not, that is, its bodily and mental sheaths, is held to be responsible for all the sorrows and sufferings of human life, because the Self wrongly imagines that various affections and afflictions which really belong to the body-mind complex are aspects of its own nature. Only when the *Ātman* is able to abstract itself from these sheaths by a long and rigorous spiritual training under the guidance of a Guru or spiritual guide does it shine forth in its pristine divine glory as the same with God (*Brahman*). But so long as this does not happen the Self suffers from the illusion that it is subject to all the evils, imperfections and limitations of its external sheaths and thus makes itself a miserable victim of the distressing sense of finitude, suffering and death.

But at the same time the fact that each conscious individual instinctively desires to escape suffering and resist death proves that this miserable and wretched existence is neither one's essential nature nor final destiny. For if some foreign element enters our body, such as a particle of dust in the eye or a thorn in the flesh, the body immediately reacts to it and tries to rid itself of it; likewise, every person wants to get rid of the sorrows and sufferings of human life, which therefore shows that these do not belong to the essence of the Self but are foreign elements which have become imposed on it. This suggests again that the natural condition of the Self is a state of perfect and unalloyed peace or bliss (*ānanda*) absolutely free from all sufferings and imperfections. This painless perfect state of the Self has been variously termed in the Upanisads *mukti, moksa, kaivalya, apavarga*, and so on, and the attainment of this state is described as the supreme end of human life (*carana purusārtha*).

But how is one to attain this ideal state? Only by tearing off the veil of cosmic nescience (*avidyā*) and thus realizing the essential identity of one's inner Self with Brahman: this is the invariable answer of the Upanisads. When one realizes this identity one knows the truth that 'the Self is free from evil, free from old age, free from death, free from grief, hunger and thirst. . .,[9] that is free from all temporality, affections and afflictions of body and mind. That is why humans are described in the Upanisads as the 'sons of Immortality' (*amrtasya putrāh*).

This doctrine of the essential identity of the human Self (*Ātman*) with God (*Brahman*) represents the central spiritual insight of the Vedic-Upanisadic seers and gives Hinduism its distinctive character. It is interesting to note here that this ancient Upanisadic doctrine of *Ātman-Brahman* identity finds a parallel expression in the medieval Christian mystic Eckhart: 'To gauge the Soul we must gauge it with God, for the Ground of God and the Ground of the Soul are one and the same'.[10] To know the Self, therefore, is to know God: and to know God is to know everything, because everything in the Universe is pervaded by God, 'all this is enveloped by God'.[11] Thus the strange question – what is that which, being known, everything else becomes known? – finds its answer in the human Self: *Ātmānam Viddhi*: 'know your own Self'. It is for this reason that all the Upanisadic writings together go by the name, *ātmavidyā*, a study of the nature of the Self.

THE STATUS OF MINOR GODS (DEVAS) IN HINDUISM

As the Upanisads are called *ātmavidyā*, so the Samhitās, the first and oldest part of the Vedas, may aptly be designated as *devavidyā*, a study of the nature of gods, because these are collections of hymns and prayers addressed to different gods, or the *devas* as they are called. A particular Rg-Vedic verse (VIII.28.1) and the traditional commentaries on the Vedas allude to 33 such *devas*, viz. Indra, Varuna, Usha, Agni, and so on. These gods are said to be the supernatural and luminous[12] personalities through whose active agency and guidance different objects of nature and phenomena are able to function. Understood in this sense Indra is the god of rain, thunder and storm, Varuna the god of sky, Usha the goddess of dawn, Agni the deity of fire, and so on. Though the relation of these Vedic gods with nature is very intimately conceived, they are not mere natural forces *personified*, as often interpreted by Western scholars. It would be truer to understand them as *personalities* presiding over different phenomena of nature (*abhimāna-devatās*) and guiding and controlling them. Prayers for favour could be addressed to them, for they were deities more powerful than ourselves and had control over nature, and as personalities they could be gracious.

But a very crucial question which we have already raised immediately crops up here: how can the existence of many gods (*devas*), as we find it in the Samhitā portion of the Vedas, be reconciled with the basic Upanisadic doctrine that God (*Brahman*) is one and only one and that the individual Self (*Ātman*) is essentially identical with God? Unless this question is satisfactorily answered, a critic of Hinduism might argue, the entire bulk of Vedic literature on which Hinduism is based remains a senseless mumbo-jumbo of irreconcilable contradictions.

To an objection of this kind a typical Hindu reply would be that there is no pure and unmixed polytheism in Hinduism. What appears to be polytheism in the verses of the Samhitās is really monotheism, only clothed in polytheistic guise. This leads us to a more basic enquiry into the nature of the existence of these Vedic deities (*devas*) and their metaphysical status.

If we take the pre-Christian pagan religion of the classical Greeks and the Romans to be typical examples of pure polytheism, it is not difficult to see why Hinduism cannot be subsumed under this category. In Graeco-Roman paganism the main difference between gods and humans is that the former are immortal while the latter are not, and a mortal can never attain to the status of a god. But in Hinduism humans and gods share a common fate in that both are created by an omnipotent creator God and as creatures both are subject to birth and death. Like human beings, the destiny of these gods is determined by the karmic law of cause and effect, and this law sets a beginning and an end to their status as gods. In accordance with the law of *karma*, a pervasive assumption in Indian religio-philosophical thought, the joys and sufferings of human life are strictly conditioned by and proportionate to the merits (*punyas*) and demerits (*pāpas*) of actions (*karmas*) performed by the individual: virtuous actions are rewarded by appropriate happiness and evil deeds are punished by befitting misery. Now if the merits of actions earned by someone are of such immense magnitude that all earthly pleasures are too paltry to provide rewards proportionate to these merits, then after physical death he or she is reborn as a god (*deva*) in heaven to enjoy uninterrupted heavenly bliss, and remains there as an extraordinarily powerful being to govern certain courses of nature. Unmixed pleasure and superhuman power characterize the lives of these heavenly gods. Again, when someone dies who has acquired the highest merit by performing some special kinds of penance and Vedic sacrifice (*yajña*), that person is reborn again not only as a god but as the king of gods, Indra, whose commands the lesser gods obey. But the lives of all these gods including Indra come to a definite end when their accumulated merits become exhausted by the enjoyment of heavenly pleasures and privileges; and after that they have to die from heaven as gods and be reborn again on earth as ordinary human beings within the process of repeated reincarnations known as *samsāra*. This cycle of births and deaths, either as humans or gods, goes on until they realize their essential identity with *Brahman*.

It is interesting to note here that these Vedic gods are declared to be cosmic officials holding certain positions (*padas*) and having certain duties. Thus the term 'Indra', the king of gods, is not the name of a person but designates an office or a post (*Indra-pada*). Anyone who has rendered oneself worthy of it by virtue of meritorious deeds becomes entitled to this post and occupies it. But when the merits of these good *karmas* are exhausted, one has to abdicate this office and another Indra at once steps into one's place. Thus, though these godly offices (*padas*) are constant, the individual beings that carry out the duties of Indra, Agni and the rest change.

Now considering these two peculiarities of the Vedic gods – their mortality and the ability of humans to rise to the status of gods – it is not permissible to equate the so-called Vedic polytheism with the pure polytheism of the ancient Greeks and Romans. But the most important feature to be noticed about these Vedic gods is that, though they are powerful enough to control the forces of nature and to some extent the destiny of worldly individuals, they are never described as creators of humanity and nature. Creatorship in Hinduism is an exclusive property of an Omnipotent God (*Īśvara*) who is one and uncreated. The gods (*devas*) of the Hindu pantheon correspond rather to the angels and saints and share the feature of not having possessed their high status from all eternity. The angels were created by God at the time of creation; saints attained to sainthood only after their lives on earth. The difference, however, is that unlike angels and saints these Vedic deities (*devas*) lose their status again at a later stage, whereas the former retain it by divine decree for all time. Technically, the angels and saints are sempiternal creatures, that is, they have a beginning but (apart from divine annihilation) no end. And just as the introduction of a variety of these sempiternal beings does not affect the fundamental monotheism of Christianity, so the existence of different gods (*devas*) does not in any way deprive the 'One God' theory of the Upanisads of its basic monotheistic character.

But this is not the whole story concerning the Vedic gods, and Hinduism has gone much deeper than this in its treatment of them. Among the great variety of gods it has discovered a fundamental unity, a unity which has prevented it from degenerating into a crude form of polytheism. This point has been made abundantly clear by Swami Vivekananda, a saint and savant of Hinduism, in a comparative study of other non-Hindu polytheistic mythologies.[13] In these mythologies, says Vivekananda, it is usually found that one particular god competes with other gods, becoming prominent and assuming the supreme position over others, while the other gods gradually die out. Thus, in the Jewish mythology, Jehovah becomes supreme of all the Molochs, and the other Molochs are forgotten or lost forever; Jehovah becomes the God of gods. In the same way, in Greek mythology, Zeus comes to the forefront and assumes a great magnitude, becoming the God of the Universe, and all the other gods are degraded into minor angels. This seems to be a worldwide process. But in the Hindu polytheistic mythology we find an exception. Among the Vedic gods any one is raised to the status of the

Omnipotent God for the time being when that god is praised and worshipped by the Vedic sages. Thus, when Indra is worshipped it is said that he is the all-powerful and all-knowing Supreme Lord, and the other gods, like Baruna, Ushā, Agni and so forth, only obey his commands. But in the next book of the same Veda, or sometimes in the same book, when hymns are addressed to Varuna it is said that he is the Almighty and Omniscient God, and Indra and others only obey his command. In this way all other gods occupy the position of the Supreme Lord of all in turns. Observing this peculiarity of the Vedic pantheon, Professor Max Müller, instead of characterizing the Vedic faith as polytheism, coined a new name for it and called it 'henotheism'. But to give a new name to a new situation does not explain the situation itself. Hence Max Müller's use of the new term 'henotheism' instead of polytheism does not really explain why the different Vedic gods are elevated one after another to assume the status of Almighty and Omniscient God of the Universe. The explanation, however, is there in the Vedic texts themselves. It has been expressly stated in one of the hymns of the Vedas: *Ekam sat viprā vahudhā vadanti*[14] – 'That which exists is one: sages call It by various names'. Hence only the names or concepts of gods are different, but the Reality underlying these concepts is one and the same. Multiple ways of conceiving Reality are not incompatible with the unity of the Reality conceived. Varying degrees of intellectual capacity of different individuals in apprehending one and the same Reality result in the formation of various concepts of gods. But at the heart of all these variations the same Reality reigns: 'That which exists is one: sages call it by various names'. And this is obviously not polytheism. What appears to be polytheism in the Saṁhitā portion of the Vedas is really monotheism, only dressed in polytheistic language. And though the language of polytheism clamours to draw our attention in these Saṁhitā verses, whispering notes of monotheism are not altogether absent in them, as is evident from the Gāyatri verse of the Rg-Veda already quoted. This undercurrent of monotheism in the first and oldest part of the Vedas, that is, the Saṁhitās, becomes dominant in the Upanisads of a later period when the Upanisadic sage declares in unequivocal terms: *Ekam eva advitīyam* – 'There is but One Being, not a second'. This 'One-God' theory, therefore, is the uncompromising creed of the Vedas, and the Hindu concept of God should be divined in terms of it. Hinduism has never been a pure polytheistic religion.

THE IMMANENT AND TRANSCENDENT ASPECTS OF GOD

Though God is one and only one in Hinduism, God's nature has been conceived in the Vedas in two different aspects – immanent and transcendent. In the immanent aspect God is said to be creator, preserver and destroyer of the world (*srsti-sthiti pralaya kartā*). The notion of a Creator God constitutes a fundamental category in almost all the major religious traditions of the world, and Hinduism is no exception. But one distinctive feature of the Hindu conception of the Creator God lies in that, after creating the world, God does not stand outside but remains within it. The concept of a God residing in Heaven above the universe and occasionally interfering with the affairs of the world at moments of crisis is quite alien to the Hindu mind. God, according to Hinduism, remains in the very bosom of the Universe, pervades and permeates the whole of it, and controls it while remaining within it.[15] Hence God has been described in the Hindu scriptures as the inherent creator and inner controller of the world, or the *Antaryāmin*. To appreciate properly why God is said to be inherently embedded in the Universe we need to understand the Hindu theory of creation, a detailed discussion of which is reserved for the next section. However, for the present purpose it is sufficient to note that God in the immanent aspect is no other than the Personal God of religion who, in the later Bhakti cult of Hinduism, has been invested with six attributes, viz., majesty (*aiśvarya*), omnipotence (*vîrya*), glory (*yaśa*), beauty (*srî*), knowledge (*jñāna*), and dispassion (*vairāgya*). This immanent God with attributes (*saguna Brahman*), who can be worshipped and prayed to, is specifically termed *Īśvara* in the Upanisadic literature.

But though God resides within the world and pervades the whole of it, God's being is not wholly exhausted in it; God is also beyond the world. God is both immanent and transcendent in relation to the world. This is suggested by a famous hymn of the Rg-Veda known as Purusa-sukta: 'God pervades the whole world by a quarter of His being, while the three fourth of Him stands over as immortal in the sky'.[16] The language of this hymn is of course metaphorical: we shall see later that God in the transcendental aspect defies all human measurement – both in terms of quality and quantity. But what it really suggests is that God's being cannot be unresidually equated with the world, that God is not merely the totality of the objects of the world but something more: God is also beyond the world. This 'beyond-aspect' of God is called *Brahman* just as God's immanent aspect is known as Īśvara in the Upanisads. Not only in the Rg-Veda but in other Hindu scriptures also the concept of God as 'beyond' is repeatedly emphasized.[17]

Now, from God's transcendence follows God's necessary inaccessibility to the human mind and to linguistic description. To quote from an Upanisad: *Brahman* is that 'from where mind and speech recoil, baffled in their quest'.[18] Since *Brahman* transcends the limits of all phenomenality, the concepts of our discursive reason and the words of our language through the instrumentality of which we interpret the phenomenal world do not have any legitimate application: and any attempt to apply these to *Brahman* will distort and falsify the nature of *Brahman*. Hence conceptual thought cannot grasp the real nature of *Brahman*, nor can language describe *Brahman* by any positive terms. *Brahman* can only be described negatively as 'not this, not this' (*neti neti*).[19]

But a long process of spiritual practice (*Yoga*) is able to free our minds from these concepts and transform our discursive reason into a direct state of transcendental intuition. This transformed, deconceptualized state of our minds is known as *samādhi* in the *Yoga-Sūtra* of Patanjali, and it is said that the knowledge of the true nature of *Brahman* dawns in this state. In the light of such intuitive transcendental experience (*samādhi*), the Upanisads describe the essential nature of *Brahman* as pure existence, consciousness and bliss (*sat-cit-ānanda*). Yet all these references of the scriptures do not and cannot describe the real nature of *Brahman*. These are at best suggestive hints of the great Transcendent Reality. All that we may gather from these is that *Brahman* is not void or blank (*śūnya*), nor an insentient something, but that *Brahman* is the source and support of every object and experience in nature; One without a second.

This *Brahman* when conceived as the creative energy (*śakti*) of the Universe is called Īśvara, and there is no substantial difference between the two. In fact Īśvara is the highest possible reading of the *Brahman* by the finite human mind; but beyond that mental measurement God stands as the highest, transcendental and impersonal Absolute which, however, is too much an abstraction to be loved and worshipped. So a religious devotee chooses the immanent aspect of God in order to establish a personal relationship. Thus, from the religious point of view, the concept of Īśvara is more important than the concept of *Brahman*. In the concluding section of this chapter let us concentrate on this and see in what sense Īśvara is said to be the creator and destroyer of the world.

GOD (ĪŚVARA) AND CREATION

The Vedic-Upanisadic theory of creation rests on the explicit rejection of two other rival theories – creation *ex nihilo* and creation out
of the pre-existing materials of the Universe. According to the
former theory, nothing but God existed before creation and God
created the universe out of nothing by sheer creative will. We find
this theory of creation being mentioned and rejected in one of the
principal Upanisads, and the argument on the strength of which it is
rejected is that an existent entity can never be produced out of
nothing (*kathamasatah sajjāyeteti*).[20] This argument rests on a particular view of causation known as *sat-kārya-vāda* in the Samkhya
system of Hindu philosophy.[21] According to it the effect (*kārya*)
must exist (*sat*) in its material cause in an extremely rarefied form
before it is actually produced. One gets oil from seeds, because oil is
somehow contained within the seeds before these are squeezed and
crushed. A thousand efforts on the part of the agent will not
produce a single drop of oil from the crushing of sand, because sand
does not already contain oil. Hence what is called production or
creation really means the evolution of a thing which was already
involved in its material cause. What was involved becomes evolved;
what was enveloped becomes developed; what was latent becomes
patent; and this is all that creation means in Hinduism. Hence a
thing cannot be created or produced out of sheer 'nothing' in which
it was not involved before. To say, therefore that God created the
world *ex-nihilo* is to flout this fundamental principle of creation.

    As an antidote to this theory, another theory of creation is put
forward by some cosmologists and philosophers which may be
designated as the 'Design' theory of the world. According to this
theory, God created the universe not out of sheer nothing but out of
pre-existing materials like atoms (*paramānus*), space (*dik*), time (*kāli*)
and so on, which are co-eval entities with God. These materials were
already present before and outside God, and God as a conscious
efficient agent merely shaped or designed the world out of them. On
this theory God is not so much a creator as a designer or architect of
the Universe. But Hinduism rejects this theory, finding it as faulty as
the theory of creation *ex nihilo*. The chief defect of this theory is that it
reduces God to a dependent, limited and finite being. An architect
has to depend on the materials available and can only do what these
materials make possible. In this way God becomes restricted by the
materials of creation, and God's omnipotence is lost. Thus, though

the Design theory avoids the defects of the *ex-nihilo* theory of creation, it does so at the cost of an omnipotent God. Hence it cannot be accepted as a satisfactory solution to the problem of creation.

Having rejected these two extreme views, Upanisadic Hinduism puts forward its own theory of creation in positive terms. According to it, God created the world not out of sheer nothingness, nor out of pre-existing materials lying outside God, but from within God. God is both the material cause and the efficient cause of the world (*abhinnanimittopadānā*). In ordinary empirical cases of production, the material cause (*upādāna kārana*) and the efficient cause (*nimitta kārana*) are two different things, and the material cause lies outside the efficient cause. In the case of the production of a clay pot, the clay out of which the pot is made is its material cause and the potter who consciously makes the pot is its efficient cause. After the pot is produced it continues to have an independent existence apart from and outside the potter. But this is not so with the creation of the world. Here God (Īsvara) is said to be both the efficient cause and the material cause of the world. God creates the world out of God's own inner nature. God is both the creator and the stuff of the world at the same time. Hence after creating the world, God does not stand outside it but is involved in every bit of it. God pervades and permeates the whole Universe, because it is God that has become the Universe; the Universe is an extension of God's own being, a projection of God's inner nature (*prakrti*). To quote from an Upanisad: 'Just as a spider throws out the web from within itself and again draws it in. . .so also does God (*aksara*) create the Universe'.[22]

Another interesting feature of the Hindu theory of creation is that created Nature is said to be eternal, without any absolute beginning and absolute end. No point in time is imaginable at which God existed but not yet a world. The world has a beginning and an end only in a relative sense, to be explained shortly. It is not that the Universe was created a few thousand years ago for the first time and that it will be destroyed forever a few thousand years hence. It is not that at a particular point of time God created the world, and since then God has been resting in peace except for occasional interference in its affairs. The creative energy is still going on; God is eternally creating and is never at rest. In the *Gitā*, Śrikrsna, who is believed by a sect of the Hindus to be the incarnation (*avatāra*) of God, declares: 'If I remain inactive for a single moment, the entire universe will fall into pieces'.[23]

But how can the idea of eternal creation without beginning and end be reconciled with the notion of cyclical dissolution of the world, or the *pralaya* as it is called in different Hindu scriptures? The answer is as follows. According to Hindu metaphysics the created universe is a mass of vibrations remaining at a certain level of frequency. But there are periods when this whole mass of vibrations becomes extremely rarefied, starts receding and finally gets re-absorbed into God from where it was projected forth. This unmoved mass of vibrations of the Universe within God is known as *pralaya* or the cosmic dissolution. But it should not be taken to mean the absolute destruction of the Universe. The Universe during *pralaya* does not explode into absolute non-being forever. Having reached the lowest level of frequency it merely exists as an unmanifested condition within God. What was evolved from God becomes again involved within God. But after a period of such temporary in-volution the whole world again evolves forward at the beginning of a new cycle. This process of involution and evolution of the world goes on backward and forward like ocean-waves through all eternity. Again this sort of *pralaya* does not take place simultaneously in all parts of the Universe. A particular solar system like ours may be disintegrating but thousands of others will continue to exist in their manifested condition. Thus creation taken as a whole is eternal in the sense that it has neither an absolute beginning nor an absolute end. Whenever in the Hindu scriptures the words 'beginning' and 'end' of the world are used, they should be taken to mean the beginning and end of one particular cycle, and no more than that.

Notes and References

1. Traditionally the Vedas are divided into four parts – Saṁhitās, Brāhmanas, Aranyakas and Upanisads. But since the Āranyakas intend to be the philosophical interpretations of Brāhmanic ritualism, these may be treated as parts of the Brāhmanas and not as a separate branch of the Vedas.
2. *Chāndogya Upaniṣad*, VI.2.1.
3. *Ṛg-Veda*, III.62.10.
4. *Atharva Veda*, XIX.7.12.
5. S. K. Chatterjee, *The Fundamentals of Hinduism* (University of Calcutta, 1970) p. 6.
6. *Chāndogya Upaniṣad*, VI.8.7.
7. *Muṇḍaka Upaniṣad*, I.1.3.
8. *Kathopaniṣad*, II.1.10.
9. *Chāndogya Upaniṣad*, VIII.7.1.

10. Quoted in Aldous Huxley, *Perennial Philosophy* (London: Chatto & Windus, 1974) p. 19.
11. *Isopaniṣad*, 1.
12. In fact the word 'deva' is derived from the Sanskrit root *div* which means 'to shine'. Thus derived, the word *devas* (gods) would etymologically mean the bright ones who shine in their glory.
13. See Swami Vivekananda, *Hinduism* (Sri Ramakrishna Math, Mylapore, Madras-4, India, 1968) pp. 23–4.
14. *Ṛg-Veda*, I.164–6.
15. *Bhagavad Gitā*, XV.13.
16. *Ṛg-Veda*, I.90.3.
17. *Bṛhadāranyaka Upaniṣad*, III.9.26; *Bhāgavad-Gitā*, X.42 and XV.16–17.
18. *Taittiriya Upaniṣad*, II.9.1.
19. *Bṛhadāranyaka Upaniṣad*, III.9.26.
20. *Chāndogya Upaniṣad*, VI.2.1–2.
21. In the Saṁkhya system elaborate arguments are given in support of this theory of causation. For an excellent summary of these arguments see S. Radhakrishan, *Indian Philosophy* (London: Allen & Unwin, 1962) Vol. II, pp. 256–8.
22. *Muṇḍaka Upaniṣad*, I.1.7.
23. *Bhāgavad-Gitā*, III.24.

12

Response to Sushanta Sen

Margaret H. Dornish

INTRODUCTORY

In initially pondering the nature of my response to Professor Sen's comprehensive discussion of what I prefer to call the Hindu concepts of God, I thought I might make the sort of remarks that an historian of religions is supposed to make: for example, raising particular questions about the manner in which Professor Sen has gone about his exegesis of the texts so as, in my view, to collapse the real tensions which exist within the Hindu tradition – and indeed within the Vedas; or his omitting to take explicit account of the manifest historical 'layering' of the tradition, as when he seems to conflate Vedic, Upanisadic and Puranic texts to seem to say essentially the same thing.

Upon further reflection, however, I felt that such a response would not do justice to Professor Sen's intent or to that of this discussion, which I take to be critical dialogue, not philology or text-criticism. And in any case, I am not a Sanskritist. Accordingly, my written response is confined to a discussion of only some of the content of the previous chapter. However, I hope he and others will take up the issue of the Upanisadic axiom that whatever changes cannot have any intrinsic value and reality of its own, since much in the fully developed tradition, especially in the mythology, seems to contradict this presupposition. Also, I would hope for further remarks by Professor Sen on the, as I see it, 'non-moksa' orientation suggested in his final section on the repeated creation, dissolution and re-creation of the world(s) out of God. How specifically would he relate the notion that whatever undergoes change cannot be fully real (the basis of the moksa enterprise) with this later (Puranic) notion of the God who is periodically in motion and at rest (the structure of evolution and involution)? That is to say, the world view preserved in the *Rg-Veda*, in the *Bhagavad-Gītā*, and in many Puranas holds that worldly life (saṃsāra) is real and good; the world view that first appears in the Upaniṣads holds that saṃsāra is not good (and only more or less 'real') and that the wise person seeks *only* release. What is humanly good in the world of continuous involution/ evolution?

It is not only the image-making capacity of the Hindu imagination that confronts the Western student of Hinduism, but the bold Hindu polytheistic consciousness. Here too, in attempting to understand another culture, we discover one of the great myths of our own: the myth of monotheism. Myths are those 'stories' we pre-suppose about the nature of the world and its structures of meaning. Usually we take our own myths so much for granted that it is striking to recognize them as 'myths' which have shaped not only our religious viewpoint, but our ways of knowing. Even Westerners who consider themselves to be secular participate in the myth of monotheism: that in matters of ultimate importance, there in only One – one God, one Book, one Son, one Church, one Seal of the Prophets, one Nation under God. The psychologist James Hillman speaks of a 'monotheism of consciousness' which has shaped our very habits of thinking, so that the autonomous, univocal, and independent personality is considered healthy; single-minded decision-making is considered a strength; and the concept of the independent ego as 'number one' is considered normal.

In entering the Hindu world, one confronts a way of thinking which one might call 'radically polytheistic,' and if there is any 'great divide' between the traditions of India and those of the West, it is in just this fact (Diana L. Eck, *Darśan, Seeing the Divine Image in India*, p. 17).

I

I begin my own response to Professor Sen's chapter with this lengthy and suggestive quotation from Diana Eck's recent monograph, *Darśan, Seeing the Divine Image in India*, because in this passage she raises, disarmingly, several of the issues we find discussed by him and which are germane to the subject of this debate, perhaps most especially to those participants who find John Hick's 'hypothesis' viable (see below, 'The Real and Its Personae and Impersonae').

Of course, Hinduism has, as Professor Sen demonstrates, also affirmed Oneness as profoundly as any religion ever has. My point in introducing this quotation is to suggest that Hinduism's affirmation of Oneness has been made in a context quite different from that of the Western 'myth of monotheism'. As Eck goes on to state: 'India's affirmation of Oneness is made in a context that affirms with equal vehemence the multitude of ways in which human beings have seen that Oneness and expressed their vision. . . . The statement that "God is One" does not mean the same thing in India and the West' (p. 17).

It is along these lines that I would question Professor Sen's argument to the effect that 'what appears to be polytheism in the verses of the Saṁhitās is really monotheism, only clothed in polytheistic guise', not only on historical grounds but also on hermeneutical grounds. Moreover, I would want to argue for the religious and philosophical tradition as a whole, and as a living (hence changing) tradition, that Hindu thought is most distinctive not for its 'monism' or indeed 'monotheism' but rather for its refusal, as it were, to make the many and the one into contradictory opposites. On this point, Professor Sen does state in his discussion of the status of minor gods – with reference to the Ṛg-Vedic affirmation, 'that which exists is one: sages call it by various names' – that 'multiple ways of conceiving Reality are not incompatible with the unity of the Reality conceived'. I, however, would want to nuance this statement rather differently, in the manner I have been suggesting; that is, by giving a religiously *positive* meaning to the expression of many names and forms of the Real. They are experientially and theoretically illuminating. Professor Sen attributes multiplicity of perception and conception rather negatively as a (mal-) function of 'varying degrees of intellectual capacity of different individuals'. Such a position appears often enough in the tradition to be sure, but always in polemical or apologetic situations. A more satisfactory position, it seems to me, has been advanced by Indologist Betty Heimann:

Whatever man sees, has seen or will see, is just one facet only of a crystal. Each of these facets from its due angle provides a correct viewpoint, but none of them alone gives a true all-comprehensive picture. Each serves in its proper place to grasp the whole, and all of them combined come nearer to its full grasp. However, even the sum of them all does not exhaust all hidden possibilities of approach. (*Facets of Indian Thought*, pp. 21–2)

The interpretation given here is of facets reflecting correctly but not exhaustively, or to state the matter in another way – the Real is not only 'neti, neti' (not this, not this) but also 'it is this, it is this'. This view is congenial to Professor Sen's statement already quoted (multiple ways of conceiving Reality are not incompatible with the unity of the Reality conceived), but not to the assumption implicit throughout his prior discussion of the Brahman-Ātman identity that multiple ways are simply erroneous, false.

II

On points then, Professor Sen seems to stand for the position that the perception and/or knowledge of the one is a higher vision of the truth than either the perception of the many or the perception of the one as a complex whole (certainly the position taken in *some* Upanisads). This position, as I understand it, is that of Advaita Vedānta, set forth most compellingly by Śankara. The question I would raise here has, Hindu style, several facets. Would it not be fairer to the philosophical tradition to mention the 'modified' Vedantic theology of, for example, Rāmānuja? Rāmānuja also claims, like Śankara, that he is faithfully expounding the (same) authoritative texts (the Upanisads, the Gītā and the Brahma Sūtras – note not the Samhitās).

According to Rāmānuja, there are *three* primary kinds of being – God (Brahman), selves/souls (ātman), and inanimate matter. All three are real, since for Rāmānuja whatever is cognized is real. Selves and matter are, however, *dependent* on God. He further asserts that the highest Brahman is identical with Īśvara, not simply 'the highest reading of Brahman'; there is no 'real' distinction between quality-less (*nirguna*) and with qualities (*saguna*). Selves and matter make up the form, or body, of God. They are a manifestation of Brahman's power, which he exercises for 'sport' (*līla*), but the selves do exist in their own right and by their own nature. As the ātman rules the material body, so God rules his body (= souls and matter). Hence liberation is not the realization of the ātman's identity with Brahman, but is rather becoming *like* God and participating in the majesty of God. Moreover, although liberation may be earned in this life it is attained only at death.

In Rāmānuja's system, the world and the selves are real even though they are dependent on Brahman. As I understand it, he explains the relation between Brahman and the world in terms similar to those I have suggested describe the Hindu tradition – as parts of a whole. Similarly, too, he builds diversity into the unities he affirms; he refuses to create the problems that would force him to divorce the many from the Real.

III

I mentioned that Rāmānuja bases his theology/philosophy on the same texts as Śankara. Śankara chose a few radically monistic statements in the Upanisads as expressing the real intention of 'the Vedas', and interpreted all other passages so as to agree with these sayings. In turn, Rāmānuja repudiated this principle, taking the position that all passages in the primary scripture are equally authoritative and that Śankara's principle was an arbitrary one not given in the scriptures themselves. Of course, Rāmānuja's position is as vulnerable to criticism from another point of view as is Śankara's – it is just as arbitrary to treat all passages equally as to give special authority to a few. Professor Sen's position in isolating the 'essential teachings of the Vedas' seems to be vulnerable in the same way as Śankara's is.

While it may be the case that Advaita Vedānta has dominated Indian philosophy since the late classical period, it hardly exhausts Indian philosophy. Of course, Advaitins take quite seriously the Upanisadic saying that 'He goes from death to death who sees anything like diversity here' (*Katha Upanisad*, 2.1.11), and they typically have spared no pains to explain away the manifest diversity of Indian philosophy. They have exhausted, as it were, their problematic. Certain neo-Advaitins are attempting in creative ways to resuscitate this philosophical tradition, I understand, perhaps Radhakrishnan most notably during his lengthy career. The classic Advaitin strategy, however, denies historical development out of hand, thus obscuring the diversity of thought which 'is there' and also the impressive epistemological 'progress' of Indian philosophy.

The difficulty I am pointing to is perhaps common to all scripture-based philosophies to a greater or lesser degree. (Within the larger Indian context, however, Buddhism's concept of *upāya* – skill in means – provided a legitimate source for continual, critical re-statements of the essence of the teachings of the Buddha.)

Also, the historical Hindu tradition's apparent resolution of the problem in accepting six 'orthodoxies' seems to me a sort of corrective to Advaitic intellectual imperialism. The six orthodoxies are *darśanas,* seeings of the truth. Each has its own starting point, its own theory of causation, its own enumeration of the means by which one can arrive at valid knowledge. What they share in common, besides 'unqualified faith in the truth of the Vedas', is a common goal – liberation. Philosophical discourse can, therefore, take the form of an ongoing dialogue, in which the views of others are to be explained so that one can counter them with one's own view. Yet any point of view implicitly assumes that another point of view *is possible,* not simply false. While hardly a doctrine of progressive revelation, which faith in the infallibility and completeness of the Vedas cannot permit, it has in the past 'worked' as a theory that accomplished something like what John Hick has proposed below in chapter 20.

13

A Rejoinder to Professor Dornish's Response

Sushanta Sen

I

The main thrust of Professor Margaret Dornish's response to my paper seems to rest upon her observation that I have tried to interpret the Vedic-Upanisadic concept of *Brahman* (the Highest God) in the light of the absolutistic 'Advaita Vedanta, set forth most compellingly by Śankara', while ignoring the theistic trend of Vedanta or 'the modified Vedantic theology of Ramanuja', as she prefers to call it. The classic Advaitin strategy, opines Professor Dornish, 'obscures the diversity of thought' because it upholds the position that 'multiple ways are *simply* erroneous, false' (italics mine). 'In Ramanuja's system', on the other hand, 'the world and the selves are real even though they are dependent on Brahman', and she prefers Ramanuja's interpretation of the Upanisadic concept of Brahman to that of Śankara's.

My response to this is that my exposition was meant to be written from Śankara's point of view because, in my opinion, Śankara's philosophical system provides a broad framework which is capable of accommodating all possible ways of interpreting the Upanisadic texts. The limited space available to me did not allow me to spell out the technical connotation of some of the important terms used by Śankara, viz., the real (*sat*), falsity (*mithyā*), unity (*ekam*) and so on. To explain them here will, I think, answer some of the objections raised by Professor Dornish.

II

Śankara himself recognizes that there are two streams of thought in the Upaniṣads – absolutist and theist. The former represents the

104

ultimate reality as a qualityless impersonal being (*nirguna Brahman*) manifesting itself as the changing world of diversity and as innumerable individual selves (*jivas*), both of which are unreal or false (*mithyā*) in a highly technical sense to be explained shortly. The latter theist stream of thought holds that the ultimate reality is a personal God invested with divine qualities (*saguna Brahman*), and the world and the selves (*jivas*) are real, though dependent on *Brahman*. But according to Śankara the theistic trend in the Upanisads which affirms the diversity of worldly objects and individual selves as real is only a concession to our empirical mode of perception (*vyavahārika drṣti*). Since all duality or diversity is only conditionally true, the real teaching of the Upanisads is that of unity: 'There is but *one* being, not a second' (*Ekam eva advitiyam*) – as the Upanisads categorically put it. In this Upanisadic aphorism the meaning of the word 'One' (*ekam*) is 'the negation of the two' (*advitīyam*). In other words, the notion of unity is not a ready-made abstract concept which is directly given to our consciousness; rather, it emerges out of a cancellation of the notion of diversity which includes duality. Śankara thus holds that the knowledge of the underlying unity of the world which is no other than *nirguna Brahman* reveals itself to us in a transcendental vision (*paramārthika drṣti*) only after the experientially given world of diversity somehow gets cancelled (*vādhita*). This is precisely the reason why Śankara does not designate his system of thought as 'pure monism' (*sattādvaita*) but as 'non-dualism' (*advaita*).

The Ultimate Reality (*Brahman*), according to Śankara, is neither one nor many. It transcends both unity and plurality, and at the same time explains both. To cite an illustration from the Upanisads, Brahman is like the sun which explains the phenomena of day and night, and at the same time transcends them in that it knows no night nor day in our sense of the term. Strictly speaking, it is therefore wrong to say that Śankara teaches *bare unity*. If interpreted in this way, Professor Dornish is correct in her observation that 'Hindu thought is most distinctive not for its "monism" or indeed "monotheism" but for its refusal, as it were, to make the many and the one into contradictory opposites'. But despite this very relevant observation, Professor Dornish still finds a real contradiction between the Rg-Vedic-Purānic World view, which affirms that 'the worldly life (*samsāra*) is real and good' and the Upanisadic axiom that 'whatever changes cannot have any *intrinsic* value and reality of its own' (italics mine). A follower of Śankara, however, would answer that the world of diversity is certainly real from the empirical point of view (*vyavahārika dṛṣṭi*), as it is an experientially given fact (*prasiddha*) and nobody can deny the reality of the 'given'. One has to start *initially* with this experience of diversity only to reject or transcend it *ultimately* in order to get a transcendental vision (*pāra-mārthika dṛṣṭi*) of *Brahman*. Though *Brahman*, according to Śaṅkara, does not really possess any attribute of its own (*nirguna*), its presence can be *indicated* by some ascribed empirical marks (*tatastha lakṣaṇas*), viz., reality, unity, goodness, motion, and so on. But the true nature (*svarūpa lakṣaṇa*) of *Brahman* can be revealed to us only by the removal of these ascriptions (*adhyāropavāda nyāya*) – by *di*scovering, *un*covering, *re*moving these superimposed characters. By ascribing a mark to the Real, we in a sense negate the Real. But by negating this negation (*neti, neti*), we get back the true nature of the Real. The experience of the changing world of diversity thus serves a purpose; it is instrumental to the knowledge of *Brahman*, and in this sense it has a value and reality of its own, though this is not intrinsic but instrumental in nature.

III

It is true that Śaṅkara brands all duality – the duality of God and the world, of worldly objects and the individual selves – as illusion or false (*mithyā*). But it is not '*simply* erroneous, false' (italics mine) as pointed out by Professor Dornish. Śaṅkara uses the word 'false,' 'illusion' or 'error' (*mithyā*) in a highly technical sense, and it is important to grasp correctly the true import of this word in interpreting his thought. It is further important to bear in mind that the meaning of the falsity of the individual selves (*jivas*) is different from the so-called illusoriness (*māyā*) of the world.

Śaṅkara's conception of the Real (*sat*) is the Eternal Being (*Brahman*) which cannot be negated in the three periods of time, past, present and future (*trikāla avādhitatva*); and his conception of the unreal (*asat*) is that of absolute nothingness like a 'square-circle' a 'barren mother's child' and so on, which cannot even appear to our consciousness. Now Śaṅkara thinks that the world, in all its variety, does not belong to either of these categories. The world cannot be absolutely real (*sat*), because it is cancelled or negated to a *jivanmukta* (a living liberated soul after the realization of *Brahman* in a trans-cendental vision (*pāramārthika dṛṣṭi*)). Again, the world cannot be absolutely unreal (*asat*), like a barren mother's child, for it appears to our conscious perception. Moreover, the fact that the world has practical efficiency, being serviceable in life, also proves that it cannot be absolutely unreal. These considerations prompt Śankara to describe the world as indescribable (*anirvacanīya*) – as neither real nor unreal. In Śankara's language, though the world is an experientially given fact (*prasiddha*), yet it is not logically defensible (*siddha*), that is, it eludes any logical categorization as either real or unreal. It is in this sense that Śankara brands all duality or diversity of the world as illusion, erroneous or false (*mithyā*). Śankara himself would have readily conceded Professor Dornish's contention that many names and forms of the Real (*Brahman*) are experientially illuminating, though not theoretically or logically so. In other words, the things of the world, though not *ultimately* real, are yet of a certain order of reality. They are *appearances* in the sense that they depend for their being upon some higher reality, that is, *Brahman*. The appearance of an illusory snake in a piece of rope, for example, depends on the existence of the rope; and when this illusion is sublated, the snake as such is rejected and the reality of the rope affirmed. But this dependence in the case of the snake-rope illusion is one-sided, for while the disappearance of the rope necessarily means the disappearance of the snake, the reverse does not hold good. The same is true in regard to the relation of *Brahman* to the illusory world in the sense just explained. A liberated soul (*jivanmukta*) who has realized the ultimate Truth denies the world of change and diversity as illusion and affirms the ultimate reality of *Brahman*.

But the illusoriness of the individual soul (*jiva*) is different from the illusoriness of the world. A *jiva* is *Brahman* itself appearing through the media or limiting adjuncts (*upādhis*), such as the internal organ (*antaḥkaraṇa*), the five external sheaths (*panca-kosas*), and so on, which are all elements pertaining to the physical world and, as such, are illusory. When a *jivanmukta* (a liberated soul) realizes this in his own experience, what is denied is not the *jiva* as a spiritual entity, but only certain aspects of it, such as its finitude, its separateness from other selves, and such like. An example will perhaps make the sense clear. A person looking at a white marble icon of Lord Buddha through a sheet of yellow glass, of whose existence she is not aware, takes the icon to be yellow. But a suitable change in her standpoint will ultimately disclose to her that the yellowness belongs to the glass and not to the icon itself. It does not deny the object as such but only an aspect of it – its yellowness. The person concerned still sees it as an icon of Buddha, but only adds that it is white and not yellow. In the same way when a *jiva*, a finite individual self, realizes its identity with *Brahman*, the *jiva* is not negated in the same way as the world is negated. It is on the contrary re-affirmed, though only as *Brahman*. We cannot therefore say that the individual self (*jiva*) is illusory or false (*mithyā*) as the world is illusory. We can only say that it is not truly the agent (*kartā*), the enjoyer (*bhoktā*), and so on.

This consideration brings out exactly what is meant by the identity of the *jiva* with *Brahman*, which is of fundamental importance to the Upanisadic doctrine of God. The *jiva* is not illusory as the world is. For if the *jiva* were illusory, there would be none to be saved. Salvation implies survival. The liberated *jiva* is not totally lost in *Brahman*. But at the same time it would not be quite correct to say that it is preserved there *as it is*, for it is only *as Brahman* that it continues to be, losing its limitations (*upādhis, kosas*), which are all false. The notion of an individual self or ego (*jiva*) is thus a complex concept composed of an element which is identical with *Brahman* and of limiting adjuncts (*Upādhis*) which are illusory.

To sum up: *Brahman* is the sole reality of humanity and the Universe. The objective Universe is an illusory manifestation of *Brahman* (in the technical sense of 'illusory' explained already), while the individual subjective self (*jiva*) is *Brahman* itself appearing under the limitations (*upādhis*) which form part of the illusory Universe.

IV

It appears from her response that Professor Dornish prefers Ramanuja's Viśistādvatic interpretation of the upanisadic texts as 'a sort of corrective to Advaitic intellectual imperialism' in Śankara which, according to her, denies the objective world and the individual selves as '*simply* erroneous, false'. This is perhaps what prompts her to say that 'the Real is not only "neti, neti" (not this, not this) but also 'it is this, it is this', and this position, she opines, is not congenial to Śankara's doctrine of *Brahman-Ātman* identity. But in the light of the Advaitic interpretation of the falsity of the *jivas* offered in the previous section one can readily see that it is possible for Śankara to uphold both positions – negative (not this, not this) and positive (it is this, it is this) at the same time without any self-contradictions. A *jiva* is certainly *not identical* with its body, mind and so on, which constitute its limiting adjuncts (*upādhis*), and as such these belong to the illusory objective world. Again a *jiva* in its inner depth and dimension *is really identical* with *Brahman*. As the notion of *jiva* is a complex concept composed of two opposed elements – the temporal and the eternal – there is no self-contradiction in the position that a *jiva* is both identical and not identical with *Brahman*.

Let me conclude my discussion by pointing out a formal contradiction to which Professor Dornish's exposition of Ramanuja's thought is exposed. In one place she writes that according to Ramanuja 'the selves do exist in their own right and by their own nature' but after a few lines she adds again: 'In Ramanuja's system the world and the selves are real even though they are dependent on *Brahman*'. But one can legitimately ask here, how can the selves exist in their own right and by their own nature, if they are dependent on *Brahman*? Verily the self is dependent on *Brahman*, nay, it is *Brahman* itself (*ayam Ātmā Brahman*) – would be Śankara's reply.

Part V

14

Emptiness: Soteriology and Ethics in Mahayana Buddhism*

Christopher Ives

'Emptiness' has its true connotations in the process of salvation, and it would be a mistake to regard it as a purely intellectual concept, or to make it into a thing, and give it an ontological meaning. The relative nothing ('this is absent in that') cannot be hypostatized into an absolute nothing, into the non-existence of everything, or the denial of all reality and of all being.[1]

The search for the 'ultimate' in Mahayana Buddhism leads inevitably to emptiness (śūnyatā). Emptiness first emerges as a key Buddhist concept in the *Prajñāparamitā Sūtras* (Perfection of Wisdom Sutras), Mahayana Sanskrit writings of the 1st century BCE. On the basis of this group of sutras, the great Indian philosopher Nagarjuna (2nd century CE) gives emptiness a systematic philosophical expression. In his writings, especially the *Mūlamadhyamika-kārikās* (Stanzas on the Middle Way), Nagarjuna sets forth emptiness as a thorough-going negation of independent self-existence and a refutation of substantialist conceptual approaches to reality, with the intention of dissolving human attachment and consequent suffering. Later Mahayana thinkers develop these aspects of emptiness as an ontologically descriptive term and, more importantly, a soteriological device, a skillful means (*upayā*) of leading people beyond ignorance to liberation. It is primarily in the latter sense that emptiness functions as the 'ultimate' in Mahayana Buddhism.

The Sanskrit term śūnyatā derives from the root śvi, which means to swell. That which is swollen appears full when viewed from the outside, but is often empty within.[2] Such emptiness is not necessarily

113

negative, however, for it can function constructively, as does the hollowness that enables a temple bell to ring or a gourd to function as a water vessel. (As we will see, emptiness also refers to the metal of the bell and the walls of the gourd.) In conjunction with this connotation of the term, *śūnyatā* is also the Sanskrit word for zero, the 'empty' number in mathematics. As mathematicians well know, 'in the total (holistic) system of digits, the zero is a necessary starting point as well as conclusion. . .'.[3]

Nagarjuna draws on these connotations of *śūnyatā* in responding to *Abhidharma* Buddhist thought, especially as conveyed in the *Abhidharma Pitaka*, the 'basket' of the Pali Canon that elaborates on the ethical, psychological and ontological concepts in Gautama Buddha's talks. *Abhidharma* thinkers follow the historical Buddha in his negation of an eternal, independent self (*ātman*). They assert that the 'self' is an everchanging process, not a thing, and arises through the dependent co-origination (*pratītya-samutpāda*) of numerous *dharmas*, the physical and mental factors constituting reality. The traditional formula of dependent co-origination is, in the Buddha's words,

> When this is present, that comes to be;
>   from the arising of this, that arises.
> When this is absent, that does not come to be;
>   on the cessation of this, that ceases.[4]

To clarify the constitution of subjectivity and the emergence of ignorance and suffering, *Abhidharma* Buddhists analyze and classify the various *dharmas*, which can be 'this' or 'that' in the above formula. At times, *dharmas* are discussed as independent, atomistic entities. The *Sarvastivada* ('everything exists') school of *Abhidharma* thought argues that space and Nirvana are unconditioned *dharmas*.

Nagarjuna criticizes this hypostatization of the elementary factors or *dharmas*, labelling it a metaphysical error, a form of ignorance (*avidyā*) which conduces to attachment and further suffering. He contends that not only composite entities but also their compositional elements come into being through the interaction of various conditions in a constantly changing field of interaction. In other words, *all* things lack own-being (*svabhāva*)[5]; they are empty (*śūnya*), devoid of independent self-existence. Nagarjuna is not arguing that nothing exists or that we live in an illusory nihilistic void, but that there are no independent, unchanging, permanent essences. As he writes, 'Since there is no *dharma* whatever originating independently, no *dharma* whatever exists which is not empty'.[6] Simply put, Nagarjuna proceeds a step beyond the earlier Buddhist notion of 'personal selflessness' and expounds the 'selflessness of dharmas'. Of course, in the process he reconceptualizes the Theravadin notion of dependent co-origination, for 'in the context of emptiness (*śūnyatā*), co-originating dependently loses its meaning as the link between two "things"; rather it becomes the form for expressing the phenomenal "becoming" as the lack of any self-sufficient, independent reality'.[7] Thus Nagarjuna states, 'The "originating dependently" we call "emptiness"'.[8]

Emptiness as the negation of independent self-existence pertains not only to the human self, the array of things in our world, and the compositional factors, but to the religious ideal of *nirvāna* as well. Unlike *Sarvastivadin Abhidharma* thought, Nagarjuna does not regard *nirvāna* as an independent, unconditioned state. Convinced of universal relatedness, he considers such an independent reality a mental fabrication and argues that true *nirvāna* is not found apart from living-dying (*samsāra*), but realized in its midst:

> There is nothing whatever which differentiates the existence-in-flux (*samsāra*) from *nirvāna*;
> And there is nothing which differentiates *nirvāna* from existence-in-flux.[9]

From the standpoint of unawakened, conventional knowledge, *samsāra* and *nirvāna* are seen as thoroughly opposite, whereas in absolute knowledge they are grasped as non-dual. Further, in the realization of emptiness, one is not attached to either of the realms conceptualized in conventional knowledge: *samsāra* or *nirvāna*, the secular or the sacred. This non-attachment constitutes religious freedom. 'In the realization of emptiness through complete detachment from both the secular and the sacred worlds one can freely move back and forth between the two worlds without hindrance.'[10]

Nagarjuna even argues that emptiness itself is empty. 'Emptiness' does not refer to a transcendent, substantial Reality. As one scholar remarks, 'when emptiness is described as inexpressible, inconceivable, and devoid of designation, it does not imply that there is such a thing having these as characteristics'.[11] Again, emptiness is synonymous with dependent co-origination, with the continuous changing system of relationships called 'becoming'. It is not apart from actuality, as indicated by the famous line in the Heart Sutra, 'Form is emptiness and emptiness is form'.

Emptiness, then, is not a religious ultimate in the sense of a transcendent Being or eternal Oneness. In fact, emptiness negates the reification of *anything* as an ultimate. This point is of crucial soteriological significance. 'Only by realizing that the *dharma* [the historical Buddha's teaching], the Path, and the Buddha were not ultimate entities to be grasped by intellectual or meditative techniques could one be free from the attempt to possess an Ultimate as well as be free from the sorrow resulting from not attaining that illusory "Ultimate".'[12] Nagarjuna's articulation of emptiness thus serves to dissolve ignorant structures of experience and lead us toward a realization of liberating wisdom (*prajñā*). 'Epistemologically, emptiness is *prajñā*, an unattached insight that truth is absolutely true.'[13] But what is the nature of attachment and suffering?

As the historical Buddha discussed in his talks on the Four Holy Truths, human suffering is caused primarily by desire or craving (*tṛṣṇa*). Through ignorance (*avidyā*) of dependent co-origination and impermanence, a person takes the objectified self and other experiential objects to be independent, enduring entities, and through this mode of experience grows attached to them positively (desire and love) or negatively (aversion and hatred). This ignorance of the conditioned nature of the self and its world derives in large part from hypostatizing that which we experience and giving it a convenient designation, such as 'me', 'you', 'us', 'them', 'career', 'fame', or 'wealth'. To the degree subjectivity positions itself as some thing or self, identifies with that position and whatever bolsters it, becomes negatively attached – through aversion, fear and hatred – to entities threatening it, and works to protect and maintain its position relative to the non-self, subjectivity becomes alienated from its world, the very context and source of its be-ing. Moreover, in objectifying itself through self-consciousness, subjectivity becomes split into a reflective subject and reflected-upon object, and thus becomes estranged even from itself.[14]

To loosen attachment to the boundaries created by the 'thinking-thinging'[15] process, Nagarjuna explicates the relational character of reality. In the *Mūlamadhyamika-kārikās*, he sets forth emptiness to negate the reification of the convenient constructions (*prajñapti*) of language and the projection of them onto reality. He asserts that the so-called essence is nothing but a hypostatization of word-meaning. The word, he says, is not of such a nature that it indicates a real object. Instead of being a sure guarantee of the existence of an ontological essence, every word is itself a mere baseless mental construction whose meaning is determined by the relation in which it stands to other words. Thus the meaning of a word immediately changes as soon as the whole network of which it is but a member changes even slightly.[16]

Essentially, 'emptiness is a non-referring word about referring words'.[17] That is to say, 'Emptiness is not a term outside the expressional system, but is simply the key term within it. . . Like all other expressions, it is empty, but it has a peculiar relation within the system of designations. It symbolizes non-system, a surd within the system of constructs'.[18]

Further, through a dialectical analysis of various philosophical viewpoints, Nagarjuna demonstrates the inherent contradictions of any doctrinal standpoint that attempts to grasp reality conceptually. This analytical method is called *prasanga*, a type of *reductio ad absurdum*. One form this dialectical method takes is the negation of a tetralemma. Nagarjuna argues that a *dharma* is

neither 1. existent
   nor 2. non-existent
   nor 3. both existent and non-existent
   nor 4. neither existent nor non-existent.

This is echoed in Nagarjuna's eightfold negation:

I salute the Buddha,
The foremost of all teachers;
He has taught
The doctrine of dependent co-arising,
[The reality of all things is marked by]
No origination, no extinction;
No permanence, no impermanence;
No identity, no difference;
No arrival, no departure.[19]

In this way, Nagarjuna negates (empties) the ontological categories of being and non-being, and rejects both naive realism and nihilism. Reality eludes discursive, discriminating thought and its dualistic categories of being and non-being, subject and object, identity and difference, cause and effect. It cannot be objectified or articulated by any word, theory or thought process; any attempt to grasp it conceptually is doomed to failure and, more crucially, suffering. Again, this does not imply that there is an independent, substantial 'thing' eluding us. Rather, reality is beyond all distinctions of thing and no-thing, being and non-being, immanent and transcendent, or eternal and temporal. As the open, dynamic context of becoming, 'it' gives rise to all things, though never apart from them. Emptiness hence signifies that (1) nothing in the world has any self-existence, and (2) no concept or theory, nor the cognitive process that creates and uses it, can grasp the nature of reality.

A mere intellectual understanding of these two senses of emptiness is not sufficient to bring about a cessation of suffering, for ignorance colours not only the intellectual but also the emotional and volitional aspects of human existence. To understand emptiness non-objectively in its full religious significance, ignorant subjectivity must be sloughed off. This emptying requires more than a mere philosophical dialectic, so Nagarjuna's logic must be linked with an engaged religious quest. Through meditation and other religious practices, or through despair of the ego-self and a realization of the human predicament, one arrives at what Zen refers to as Great Doubt and Great Death, in which dualistic ego-consciousness is broken through. More specifically, subjectivity entangled in the ignorant reification and attachment process reaches an impasse and ultimately drops away, an event the Japanese Zen master Dogen (1200–1253) calls 'the dropping off of mind and body'. Simultaneously, unattached liberated subjectivity awakens. This subjectivity is not attached to or identified with any particular self-definition or form, and hence has been termed the 'Formless Self' by a modern Zen master, Shin'ichi Hisamatsu. And since emptiness understood as absolute subjectivity is beyond the grasp of language and conceptual thought, it is said to be 'unattainable' (*anupalambha*), or unobjectifiable. This aspect of emptiness generates such metaphors as a sword unable to cut itself or an eye unable to see itself while functioning effectively in actuality.

The goal of Nagarjuna's dialectic and the accompanying quest, then, is a transcendence of subjectivity that reifies things or states of affairs and becomes attached to that which has been reified. In Nagarjuna's writings and before him 'in the *Prajñāparamitā*, supreme enlightenment is identified with the attainment of *śūnyatā*. In other words, the object of the Buddhist life is to find an unattached abode in this realization. This abode is called *apratishthita*, not-abiding'.[20] In Mahayana Buddhism, non-abiding, liberated subjectivity is equipped with the wisdom (*prajñā*) that 'sees' the arising of all things in emptiness (dependent co-origination). Such wisdom does not indicate a retreat from actuality into annihilation or a void, but a dynamic realization that emptiness is none other than form, that is, the world of events. This dynamic regrasping of actuality in terms of open, processive emptiness is empowered by the energy formerly blocked in the attempt to maintain a delineated self and its boundaries. 'To maintain this integrated self, enormous *binding force*, or *clinging*, is required. Setting loose the binding force of ego-clinging thus releases the tremendous potential energy within, and this constitutes what Buddhism calls Enlightenment and liberation.'[21]

In conjunction with this transformation, subjectivity has shifted epistemologically from conventional, practical knowledge and truth (*samvṛti-satya*) in which the person was entangled, to liberated religious knowledge and truth (*paramārtha-satya*), the insight into universal emptiness. On the basis of the latter, the person is able to make use of conventional knowledge in the everyday practical realm without causing suffering by reifying the convenient concepts used in such knowledge. Epistemologically, 'all dualism or conceptual distinction is reconstructed in the realization of Emptiness without any possibility of clinging to distinction'.[22] And in making the shift to the second truth, the anxiety, pain and dis-ease previously experienced disappear as subjectivity stops clinging and opens up to empty, dependent co-arising. Paradoxically (at least when seen from our ordinary perspective), salvation is achieved not by realizing an eternal, unchanging reality outside of becoming, but by overcoming the subjectivity that seeks permanence apart from actuality and thus entering fully into becoming Here and Now. In this way, the problem of the search for permanent being outside of becoming is dissolved, rather than 'solved' through the discovery of a permanent Reality, the way normal subjectivity imagines the problem to be solvable. One's whole being shifts from substantialist, dualistic thought, to non-substantial thought, or, in the words of one Buddhist scholar, from the '*Svabhava*' way of thinking to the '*Nihsvabhava*' ('no-own-being', empty) way of thinking, as delineated in the following:

The *Svabhava* Way	The *Nihsvabhava* Way
independent	interdependent
unitary	structural
entity and substance	events and actions
static	dynamic
fixed	fluid
bound	free
definitely restricted	infinite possibilities
clinging and attachment	release and detachment
thatness	thusness[23]

It must be noted here, however, that the empty (*Nihsvabhava*) way of thinking or experiencing is not a theory advanced in opposition to theories based on substantialist *svabhavic* thought. Rather, it cuts through all cognition, all theoretical standpoints that attempt to objectify reality and grasp its nature conceptually. Emptiness serves to circumvent such thought, not to give it a correct object to ponder. Nagarjuna asks us to empty ourselves of such objectification, discrimination, and conceptualization – and then experience in terms of *prajñā*.

In addition to the critical, soteriological and epistemological aspects of the term, emptiness also plays a positive 'ontological' role in Nagarjuna's thought. To Nagarjuna, emptiness is not merely a negation of own-being (*svabhāva*), for it is only by virtue of emptiness that things can 'be'. As discussed earlier, to be is to co-originate with other things through mutual conditioning. And to be open to the various conditions, the relational entity must be *empty* of any independent, self-contained status. Thus, as one Buddhist scholar tells us, 'things exist by virtue of their true emptiness. . . . If things were not empty of a substance or essence, they could not exist even for a second; conversely, without things, there can be no emptiness. This is not hard to understand if it is remembered that emptiness refers only to the mode of being of existents'.[24] In Nagarjuna's words,

> When emptiness 'works', then everything in existence 'works'. If emptiness does not 'work', then all existence does not 'work'.[25]

Since universal interrelating provides the necessary condition for things to 'be', all apparently enduring entities (me, you, the piece of paper before us) are constantly 'open' to constitutive factors;

accordingly, an independent entity with own-being cannot even begin to exist. It is not that things exist *even though* they are empty, but that things exist *precisely because* they are empty. On this basis we express schematically the meaning of the aforementioned couplet from the Heart Sutra, 'Form is emptiness, emptiness is form':

form is emptiness   no own-being (*svabhāva*); 'things'
                     arise only through dependent co-origination

emptiness is form   the dependent co-origination by virtue of
                     which 'things' arise is not apart from them

Thus it is not the case that emptiness or dependent co-origination exists temporally or ontologically prior to actuality; rather, emptiness as dependent co-origination is the actual dynamics of reality in its very becoming.

In awakening to emptiness as the dynamics of becoming, as the mode of be-ing, we realize the convergence of ontology, epistemology and ethics. Ontologically, the emptied self ceases to posit itself as an enduring, bounded entity standing in opposition to the objects of its experience (including itself as objectified in dualistic knowing). It experiences the world as a system of dynamic, processive interrelationships (temporal) and mutual constitution (atemporal and structural in the now). More exactly, the emptied self *is* its experience. That is to say, it is not that we *have* an experience of something, but that we *are* our experience. In the immediacy of direct experience prior to later reflection, the experiencer, experiencing and experienced are not separate. Epistemologically, this openness and direct experience is *prajñā*, defined here as experiencing in the mode of emptiness, that is, nihsvabhavically. Psychologically, 'the dawning of *prajñā*, by which one sees the emptiness of things, is an act of absolute encompassing whereby one's boundaries expand to include everything. To see emptiness is to become emptiness, or, . . . to become empty is to see emptiness'.[26] To use the terminology of one Zen philosopher, this openness is the 'boundless expanse of Awakening' (*Kaku-no-hirogari*).[27] This can be understood only when the reflective, hypostatizing ('thinging') ego-self is emptied and formless subjectivity (Awakening) opens up. In Nagarjuna's parlance, this is the shift from *samvṛti-satya* to *paramārtha-satya*.

Given that the 'self' is precisely the dynamism of experiencing, human knowing and being converge. More exactly put, emptiness indicates the level at which knowing and being (and doing) are still undivided. Understood in this way, 'emptiness' functions as the ground of Mahayana Buddhist ethics. When we conceive of *śūnyatā* as 'emptying', that which is emptied is the self-centred, defensive, boundary-forming ego-self. Emptying is a liberating expansion, in which emptied subjectivity becomes a context for fullness. It is not unlike the sky, the other meaning of the Chinese ideograph for *śūnyatá*. As one Zen master states, 'We should always live in the dark, empty sky. The sky is always the sky. Even though clouds and lightning come, the sky is not disturbed'.[28]

Through this emptying of the ego-self, the artificial distinctions and discriminations made with regard to others are emptied as well. The other is now seen for what he or she is. In Buddhist terminology, the person is seen in his or her suchness, or 'as-it-is-ness'. And at a deeper level, our sense of self expands to include others. One contemporary Zen master writes,

> The practice of 'being with them' [realizing mutual constitution] converts the third person, *they, it, she, he,* into the first person *I,* and *we.* For Dogen Zenji, the others who are 'none other than myself' include mountains, rivers, and the great earth. . . .
>
> This is compassion, suffering with others. 'Dwell nowhere, and bring forth that mind' [Diamond Sutra]. 'Nowhere' is the zero of purest experience, known inwardly as fundamental peace and rest. To 'come forth' is to stand firmly and contain the myriad things.[29]

In conjunction with the realization of such subjectivity, we are emptied of rigid attachment to personal notions of truth and falsehood, right and wrong. We realize that all views, including our own, are tentative and partial. Here the road to tolerance, inclusiveness and participation opens before us, and we begin to serve each other as we inter-act and inter-create in the open context of emptiness. We shift from a svabhavic, self-centred outlook to a holistic, organic view of actuality. No longer frightened and defensive, we can act freely and creatively in the web of interrelationship. 'Not holding on to a notion of self, we are invited to engage ourselves courageously in the world, to see the nature of suffering clearly, and with discriminating awareness to undertake the task of liberating all sentient beings.'[30]

As indicated by this statement, such clear seeing (*prajñā*) is inseparable from compassion (*karunā*) and the functioning of a Bodhisattva. Emptied of the psychologically isolated and self-centred ego-self, we realize the interaction between all entities; and in this expansion of subjectivity and openness to actuality we empathically experience suffering. Entering the world of suffering, the Bodhisattva functions through various skillful means (*upayā*) to awaken others to emptiness, to liberated, unattached, boundless subjectivity. The compassionate activity realized in conjunction with liberated experiencing-being (*prajñā*) constitutes what might be called a creative expression of emptiness.

Understood as self-emptying, wisdom and compassion, emptiness points to such values as unselfishness and non-possession. By realizing interrelatedness and thereby emptying ourselves of attachment to distinctions between 'me' and 'you' or 'us' and 'them', we can begin fully to share or give of ourselves. This shift away from selfish clinging and attachment has ramifications for relationships between the Western and Eastern blocs, wealthy and impoverished nations, higher and lower socio-economic classes, the powerful and the disenfranchised, and the human and natural realms. The characteristics of unselfishness and non-possession stand in contrast to the oft-encountered emphasis on competition, control and dominance emerging from the view of people as independent selves with certain claims and possessions.

On the basis of emptiness, we can also regrasp power as a reciprocal, mutually-enabling force, not a one-way or hierarchical form of coercion. In an interview, one Buddhologist states,

> In the patriarchal, hierarchical construction of reality, you have a one-way linear causality. We've been conditioned by that notion since Aristotle, and it has dominated both religion and science. Consequently power is seen as emanating from the top down. It is essentially power-*over*, and equated with domination, having one's way, pushing things around, being invulnerable to change. Such a notion of power requires defenses, whether of the ego or the nation state.

> But in dependent co-arising, causality is not linear. Power is a two-way street. It is not power-over, but power-with, where beings mutually affect and mutually enhance each other. The old linear notion is essentially that of a zero-sum game: the more you have the less I have; 'you win, I lose.' But it is breaking down

now, as more and more folks are talking about playing a 'win-win game.' That idea is very close to synergy, which literally means power-with, and which requires no defenses because it operates through openness. This is the kind of power we find at play in an ecosystem or neural net, where open interaction is essential to skillful functioning and the arising of intelligence and beauty.[31]

Emptiness also allows for an expansion of ethics beyond the human realm to all aspects of the cosmos. Through *prajñā*, non-human sentient beings, non-conscious life forms, and inorganic natural processes in the world are experienced in their uniqueness and realized as contributory to the be-ing of oneself. This gives rise to reverent, non-violent attitudes toward the natural domain and a commitment to maintaining a healthy environment for all life forms. In this sense, awakening to emptiness grounds one in a cosmo-centric rather than an anthropocentric standpoint,[32] a standpoint with extensive implications for ecology and economics.

The realization of emptiness, then, does not lead to a static annihilation or void apart from daily living. Buddhist detachment is from the self-centred ego, not from the world. Further, it is empti-ness that makes change, freedom and creative action possible, for it breaks beyond selfishness, rigidity, intransigency and the myriad boundaries set up by human ignorance, and indicates a dynamic process of becoming in which transformation can occur. As we saw above, it is on the basis of this transformational freedom that a Bodhisattva functions to lead others beyond ignorance. Neverthe-less, for Buddhism to fully enter into the modern age as a system of transformation in the deepest sense, it must undertake the task of clarifying how a Bodhisattva's engaged salvific activity relates to social, political and economic liberation. That is to say, Buddhists must set forth how various conditions in actuality express large-scale ignorance, how such conditions affect individual and group attempts to realize political and spiritual liberation, and how Buddhism provides a basis for – and can motivate people to engage themselves in – constructive social action and liberation in all senses of the term. Approaching this task on the basis of emptiness, Mahayana Buddhists can play a greater role in the ongoing struggle for spiritual and social liberation in the modern world, and thereby express the true significance of emptiness as a religious ultimate.

Notes

*I wish to thank Professors Masao Abe and Steve Smith for their valuable suggestions at various stages of the writing of this essay.

1. Edward Conze, *Buddhist Thought in India* (Ann Arbor: University of Michigan Press, 1967) p. 61.
2. Edward Conze, *Buddhism: Its Essence and Development* (New York: Harper & Row, 1975) p. 130.
3. Kenneth K. Inada, 'The America Involvement with Sunyata', in *Buddhism and American Thinkers*, eds Kenneth K. Inada and Nolan Jacobson (Albany: State University of New York Press, 1984) p. 82.
4. David J. Kalupahana, *Buddhist Philosophy, A Historical Analysis* (Honolulu: University Press of Hawaii, 1976) p. 28.
5. According to Richard Robinson and Willard L. Johnson, *svabhāva* indicates 'something (1) existing through its own power rather than that of another, (2) possessing an invariant and inalienable mark, and (3) having an immutable essence'. *The Buddhist Religion, An Introduction*, 3rd edn (Belmont, CA: Wadsworth, 1982) p. 69.
6. *Mūlamadhyamika-kārikās*, XXIV, 19, tr., Frederick Streng, in *Emptiness, A Study in Religious Meaning* (Nashville: Abingdon, 1967) p. 213.
7. Frederick Streng, *Emptiness, A Study in Religious Meaning*, p. 63.
8. *Mūlamadhyamika-kārikās*, XXIV, 18, in Streng, p. 213.
9. Ibid., XXV, 19, in Streng, p. 217.
10. Masao Abe, 'Substance, Process, and Emptiness', *Japanese Religions*, Vol. 11 (September 1980) Nos. 2 and 3, p. 26.
11. Op. cit., Streng, p. 80.
12. Ibid., p. 158.
13. Hsueh-li Cheng, *Nagarjuna's 'Twelve Gate Treatise'* (Dordrecht, Holland: D. Reidel, 1982) p. 14.
14. See Richard DeMartino, 'The Human Situation and Zen Buddhism', in *Zen Buddhism and Psychoanalysis*, ed. Erich Fromm (New York: Harper & Row, 1970) pp. 142–77 for a detailed treatment of the bifurcation of the self.
15. Ken Wilber, *No Boundary* (Boulder, CO: Shambhala, 1981) p. 41.
16. Toshihiko Izutsu, *Toward a Philosophy of Zen Buddhism* (Boulder, CO: Prajna, 1982) pp. 105–6.
17. Douglas D. Daye, 'Major Schools of the Mahayana: Madhyamika', in *Buddhism, A Modern Perspective*, ed. Charles S. Prebish (University Park, PA: Pennsylvania State University Press, 1978) p. 92.
18. Richard H. Robinson, *Early Madhyamika in India and China* (New York: Samuel Weiser, 1978) p. 49.
19. Translated by Hsueh-li Cheng, *Nagarjuna's 'Twelve Gate Treatise'*, pp. 15–6.
20. Daisetz Teitaro Suzuki, *Studies in the Lankavatara Sutra* (London: Routledge & Kegan Paul, 1975) p. 94.
21. Garma C. C. Chang, *The Buddhist Teaching of Totality: The Philosophy of Hwa Yen Buddhism* (University Park, PA: Pennsylvania State University Press, 1971) pp. 78–9.

22. Masao Abe, 'God, Emptiness, and Ethics' (unpublished) p. 5.
23. Op. cit., Chang, p. 85, partially adapted here.
24. Francis H. Cook, *Hua-yen Buddhism, The Jewel Net of Indra* (University Park, PA: Pennsylvania State University Press, 1977) p. 102.
25. *Mūlamadhyamika-kārikās*, XXIV, 14, in Streng, p. 213.
26. Op. cit., Cook, p. 107.
27. Masao Abe coined this term to express the open, inclusive nature of Awakening.
28. Shunryu Suzuki, *Zen Mind, Beginner's Mind* (New York: John Weatherhill, 1973) p. 86.
29. Robert Aitken, *A Mind of Clover* (San Francisco: North Point, 1984) p. 173.
30. Fred Eppsteiner, 'In the Crucible: The Tiep Hien Precepts', in *The Path of Compassion, Contemporary Writings on Engaged Buddhism* (hereafter *PC*), eds Fred Eppsteiner and Dennis Maloney (Buffalo: White Pine, 1985) p. 101.
31. Joanna Macy, 'In Indra's Net: A Conversation with Joanna Macy', in *PC*, p. 106.
32. See Masao Abe, 'Dogen on Buddha Nature', *The Eastern Buddhist*, New Series, Vol. IV (May 1971) No. 1.

15

Reflections on Christopher Ives's Commentary

Francis H. Cook

My task of responding to Christopher Ives's commentary is rendered somewhat difficult because I can find practically nothing to pick apart, modify, or correct. His is an excellent presentation of the doctrine of *śūnyatā* as the Mahayana Buddhist absolute, and since he has avoided even the faintest odour of heresy, there will be no verbal burning at the stake. I wish to commend him for getting it all straight and presenting it clearly and effectively. Still, I must respond in some way. One way to respond to a presentation such as his is, I believe, to allow it to stimulate my own reflections on emptiness, particularly with regard to the existential import of the doctrine. As I read his paper and reflect on emptiness, I am guided by two related perceptions of Buddhism. The first is that all Buddhism can be summarized by the statement, 'Forget the self'. The other is that to forget the self is to become free to die and thereby free to live. The following comments may be seen as an extension of Mr Ives's view.

I begin with Mr Ives's observation that emptiness functions as the Buddhist ultimate primarily in its soteriological aspect. This is certainly what the doctrine of *śūnyatā* is all about, as are all doctrines, for the Buddha once said that just as the ocean is impregnated with the one taste of salt, so his Dharma is impregnated with the one taste of liberation. Emptiness is the key to the liberated life, and Buddhism is about liberation. And having reminded myself of this, I have to further remember that Buddhist liberation is not merely sexual liberation, or racial liberation, or economic liberation, but a total liberation which includes all of these but goes far beyond, perhaps unimaginably beyond. What does it mean to become radically liberated?

The very objective called 'liberation' implies, of course, that a present state of bondage exists. We would agree that this bondage is quite far-reaching. It includes the forms mentioned above, as well as political bondage, drug addiction, and the bondage to hurts suffered in childhood, which dog our steps and prevent us from being whole and free. It is rather sobering to contemplate the many faces of the masters who prevent us from being free. However, it is a rare person who reflects on less obvious forms of bondage. The average citizens of our republic, who can criticize their government with impunity, who can change occupations at will, and who are perfectly free to worship in their chosen houses of worship, exult in their freedom from the cruder and more obvious forms of bondage, but from a Buddhist perspective, they are still not very free. Their whole lives are dominated by relentless slavemasters, and they are not only blissfully unaware of servitude but rather cherish it.

The fundamental bondage, and that bondage which generates the others, is our deep – I would say rabid – fear of death. It is somewhat of a social *faux pas* to even mention the subject, but I think that not enough is said about death when discussing Buddhism. I believe that if we perform an adequate phenomenology of Buddhist liberation, we find that liberation is liberation to die. In attempts to understand Buddhism, we rightly focus on its concern with the problematic belief in a substantial, enduring self (*ātman*), or its criticism of our dualistic, binary structuring of experience, or the need to see our original face before our parents were even born, and the like, but what is often omitted is that the goad which drives the craving self onward in cycles of yearning and frustration is its deep fear of non-being. The innate tendency of the mind to objectify and substantialize itself would, in itself, be but a mere philosophical curiosity, an epistemological mistake, were it not for the fact that the mind-self's primary objective is to guarantee its own survival and to consequently take actions (*karma*) to ensure that viability. The Buddhist strategy has been to experience oneself as a non-self, a mere continuity of discontinuous drops of experience that arise and perish as conditions change, utterly lacking in any enduring substratum. One thus experiences oneself as fundamentally impermanent, which is to say, perpetually perishing and fundamentally perishable. As the enduring, substantial self vanishes in a stream of impermanence, so do the craving, desire and hatred and their vocal, physical and mental manifestations. This is liberation. What has occurred is that one has gained full self-knowledge of oneself as a perishing and perishable being and has overcome the need for self-preservation. One Zen master has spoken of this self-knowledge as the ability to float contentedly on the stream of impermanence.

Our deep-seated insecurity in the face of non-being can, in turn, be seen as the generating source of a number of cognitive or intellectual problems. Our mental life enslaves us also, because mental realities not only do not solve our deepest problem of insecurity, they exacerbate the problem. Buddhism sees this situation as a vicious cycle, in which our insecurity creates a craving for things which we believe will eliminate the insecurity. Next, *karma* – mental, vocal and physical acts – takes place in an attempt to achieve the security. The result always frustrates us because the security proves to be elusive. The frustration consequently intensifies the sense of insecurity, and the cycle is perpetuated. The objects of our quest for security take not only the form of tangible things such as money, physical safety and so on, but also such things as a need for respect, a craving for significance and meaning, identification with a dominant race, species or tribe, and so on. A prominent tendency is to adopt ideological or philosophical positions as absolute, because they are felt to provide a sense of importance or source of security. These ideological stances take several shapes.

They certainly include tribal or nationalistic allegiances and sentiments, pride in race or gender, anthropocentrism or speciesism, a belief in the absoluteness of moral codes, and, without doubt, religion itself. It must always be remembered that the ultimate goal of Buddhism as a religion is to free one of all adherences, including Buddhism itself, which we are told is merely a means to an end. Emptiness itself is empty, meaning, as Mr Ives rightly points out, that Buddhism ultimately takes no position at all. All positions are problematic because they are illusions and phantasmagoria to begin with and furthermore because they offer no security to the beleaguered self. So, Nāgārjuna says, 'Away with them all', not excluding the holy teachings of Buddhism.

Thus, Shin'ichi Hisamatsu's 'Formless Self', of which Mr Ives speaks, is not much of a good patriot, pious Buddhist, or anything else. As a thoroughly mature individual, the formless self in its formlessness is no longer compelled to find meaning or value in such things as nationality or species. This is why it is said to be formless. It has no specificity, no 'face'. The liberated individual thus stands alone and independent inasmuch as he or she no longer believes that such things grant security and inasmuch as he or she no longer requires security. This is why I said earlier that liberation is freedom to die; to abandon the *need* for security means to radically accept oneself as an impermanent, perishing being. To do so radically must entail freedom from the many 'isms' in which we seek safety, as well as the substance mode of thinking, dualistic organization of experience, and the like. 'Amen', says the formless self, who, with Heidegger, knows that to be truly oneself is not possible unless we are profoundly reconciled with our mortality.

The adherence to anything as absolute, or as substantially existing, then, is involvement with phantoms conjured up by the mind in its vain attempt to seize security of some kind. It is a projection of our profoundest anxiety and a misplaced trust. As such, this faith in our mental fabrications bears a strong resemblance to the bondage to the 'world and the flesh' so thoroughly condemned by the Apostle Paul in the *Book of Galatians*. His reason for such a condemnation is, at bottom, not so different from Nāgārjuna's rejection of all positions. For both, the problem with the world and the flesh – which not only includes the gross pleasures of the senses, materialism, and the like, but also all human institutions and objectives – is that they delude us into believing that they are a source of happiness and security. For Paul, this is a misplaced trust and sin, since only God provides true security. Nāgārjuna includes more than Paul does in the inventory of the flesh and the world, but for him, too, in a manner of speaking, the bondage to the world and flesh is sin if sin is a misplaced trust or faith in idols of any sort, whether the idols be wine, women and song (or wine, men and song) or the mental fabrications which we naively believe correspond to some external reality. The Buddhist condemnation of this misplaced trust is powerfully illustrated by the symbolic episode of Śākyamuni's rejection of palace pleasures and power and his subsequent home departure in search of self-understanding. The condemnation is extended and deepened in the *Prajñāpāramitā Sūtra* and in Nāgārjuna's systematization, where the condemnation is extended to our belief that the world in our head corresponds to something 'out there', and that these entities promise an escape from trivialization, meaninglessness, powerlessness, impermanence and our final fate. Thus, liberation is liberation from epistemological certitude and philosophical and religious innocence concerning the existence of even the Four Noble Truths, which include the promise of liberation. One is finally liberated when one knows that there is no liberation.

The needs and projects of the self cannot be separated from its childlike belief in its certainty of knowledge. Nāgārjuna's achievement was to call this certainty into question, and whatever he had to say about the objective world of nature served primarily to undergird his epistemological scepticism. It is this ruthless, unsentimental scepticism which is what is so fascinating about Mahayana Buddhism, what is exhilaratingly liberating about it, and what is so very modern about it. It is modern because only recently in Western thought has there come to be a similar scepticism concerning our ability to know very much. This crisis in confidence has been brilliantly described by Richard Rorty in his recent book *Philosophy and the Mirror of the Mind* – a kind of fox thrown in among the chickens – which portrays contemporary philosophy in the grips of this crisis as it becomes more and more clear that we are securely locked within our own thinking minds and can no longer convincingly argue that the concepts, categories and patterns of thought that populate minds correspond to an unimpeachably real, external, non-mental world. Derrida and others of the Deconstructionist movement have called into question our epistemological certainties in the areas of literature and philosophy. Only very recently have Western thinkers begun to speak of cognitive or epistemological 'horizons' within which we operate and beyond which we cannot look. A number of Western movements are similar in coming to appreciate and to face the consequences of a suspicion that our realities are mental ones and that these realities are relative, conditioned and limited. They are limited by a horizon of language and culture, the necessity of thinking on a binary pattern, the contextual nature of meaning, and certainly the needs of individual and collective selves.

Nāgārjuna knew all this two millennia ago and saw it as liberating. Why is it that the same knowledge causes such consternation among modern Western thinkers? Nāgārjuna appreciated this scepticism as the very key to liberation – the saving grace, so to speak – and as supremely valuable and positive in its salvific power. The Western reaction has been one of grave concern, even hostility. Witness John Searle's outrage and bafflement in the face of Derrida's deconstruction of J. L. Austin's own philosophical writings. Literary folk have likewise been scandalized at the suggestion that translation is impossible, and given the possibility that we are prisoners of a cognitive horizon, what implication does this have for our understanding of ancient religious texts? If the mind cannot be sufficiently polished in order to adequately reflect nature, of what can we finally be certain? This is a scary thought. The *Prajñāpāramitā* Scriptures warned us two thousand years ago that the perception of emptiness was enough to make the hair of the unprepared stand on end in horrified amazement. Why can't we find epistemological scepticism to be as exhilaratingly liberating as Nāgārjuna did?

I must close the circle and come back to the point I made earlier. The need for certainty, and the certainties we believe we possess, are intimately related to the insecure self . Without certainty we feel lost, impotent, endangered; and without our certainties we feel lost, impotent, endangered. The need for certainty is a need for meaning, which is always self-affirmative. If the self were contented with its own fragility and essential impermanence, it would have no need for self-affirmation or meaning. It could, in other words, live in a world lacking in meaning. If this rather hard-nosed reading of Buddhism sounds chilly and uncompromising, it is because I see Buddhism in its origins as being indeed chilly and uncompromising but having become, like other religions, I believe, comfortable and comforting, tamed, and humanized in recent centuries. But Buddhism is not, I believe, essentially a religion of comfort, nor should it have become so for the many for whom it is a source of comfort. To make Buddhism a religion of comfort is not merely an innocent, naive misinterpretation but a serious, even fatal, false step on the path of liberation, because it is a failure to grasp Buddhism's unique approach to liberation in consistently snatching away those things on which we rely for comfort, as does Paul in his letters. If even emptiness is empty and therefore nothing to rely on, how much more so are our other conceptual realities! The message of the *Prajñāpāramitā* literature is abundantly clear and unambiguous: our truths and certainties are conditioned, transient and relative, which is to say, empty. As such, they are delusory and nothing on which to rely. The ultimate truth is that there is no ultimate truth, including the notion of 'ultimate'. Awakened Ones of the past, present and future have relied on, and shall rely on, the pristine knowledge (*prajñā*) that truth, value and meaning are empty.

The Buddhist ultimate or absolute is a very strange one. In its soteriological role, its primary purpose is to demolish as really real those inhabitants of the human mind which we believe are indubitable reflections of external reality. One of these inhabitants, along with trolls, unicorns and demons, is the notion of an absolute, a *ne plus ultra* beyond (in some sense) the conditioned world of impermanence, corruption and sin, which nevertheless reflects value, significance and meaning back on our own lives. The human heart seems to need some such notion, and it is not surprising that so much ink has been expended over the centuries to prove its existence and map out its contours. It is interesting that Mahayana Buddhism escaped the temptation to demonstrate the existence of a superior ultimate which would replace the ill-conceived ultimates of competitors. Rather than offer a superior position, it offered no position. The soteriological device of emptiness is merely a surgical tool used to excise our self-serving delusions and does not itself survive the surgical operation. When all else is emptied out, it too is emptied out. *Nothing* remains. It seems to be implicit in the Mahayana strategy that absolutes are not only not required as part of a salvational system but that absolutes themselves constitute a significant part of the existential problem. Consequently, to be totally free must entail freedom from the notion of an absolute or ultimate. It is on this field of emptiness where there are no beings and no *nirvana* to which they are led that the compassionate Bodhisattva strives energetically to lead all beings to *nirvana*, but that is another story for another time.

16

Comment on Christopher Ives

Stephen T. Davis

My one comment is less about Christopher Ives's excellent exposition than about the doctrine he expounds. He tells us that the Mahayana doctrine of emptiness signifies two things:

(1) Nothing in the world has any self-existence;

and

(2) No concept or theory, nor the cognitive process that creates and uses it, can grasp the nature of reality.

Now if (2) is true, we naturally wonder how (1) can be known or even rationally believed. Doesn't (1) help us grasp the nature of reality – something (2) says we cannot do? Unless I have missed something, the two statements are simply inconsistent.

17

Response to Stephen Davis

Christopher Ives

Traditionally, Mahayana Buddhism has made the claim that our ordinary cognitive process, the 'mind' that produces the concepts and theories found in conventional knowledge, fails to grasp reality. Moreover, that process gives rise to the notion of independent 'things' and to attachment – attraction and aversion – to those reified things, which causes suffering. For these interconnected epistemological and soteriological reasons, the normal thinking 'mind' must be thoroughly negated. Upon this negation, one awakens to liberated knowledge (*paramārtha-satya*) or wisdom (*prajñā*), in which one experiences reality without the distortion caused by ordinary conceptualization. Describing reality experienced through wisdom, Mahayana Buddhists may state that 'nothing in the world has any self-existence' or that 'reality is dependent co-origination', all the while recognizing the inability of words to convey their experience adequately. On the basis of the conviction that wisdom does grasp the nature of reality but ordinary cognition and concepts do not, Zen Buddhism ultimately appeals to practice and Awakening. As Tê-shan (780–865) declared before burning his notes and commentaries on the Diamond Sutra, 'Even though one masters various profound philosophies, it is like placing a single strand of hair in the great sky; even if one gains all the essential knowledge in the world, it is like throwing a drop of water into a deep ravine' (Zenkei Shibayama, *Zen Comments on the Mumonkan*, New York: Harper & Row, 1974, p. 201).

18

Comment on Francis Cook

John Hick

Francis Cook's 'hard-nosed reading of Buddhism', and in particular of the practical meaning of śūnyatā, is extremely powerful and challenging. It does not 'leave everything as it was', in the Wittgensteinian mode, but demands a total conversion of viewpoint. Its message is, as he says, 'chilly and uncompromising'. I want to apply a questioning thermometer, not so much to measure *how* chilly it is as to see precisely *where* the chill is located. Does Buddhism present itself as the cold truth concerning the ultimate nature of reality *or* of the way in which that reality seems from our present deluded, because ego-centred, point of view?

On the one hand, the teachings of the Buddha, as reflected in the Pali scriptures, hold out the hope of *nirvāṇa*, which – whatever the word means – refers to the sought-after goal of the Noble Eightfold Path. It names a possibility for the realization of which it is worthwhile – and necessary – to give up everything else. Thus far, the Dharma would seem to be good news. On the traditional Buddhist world-view, according to which we are born again and again until at last we attain to the enlightenment which is *nirvāṇa*, the Dharma is good news for everyone; and the bodhisattva doctrine emphasizes this by telling us that the ultimate *dharma-kāya*, the Real itself, is in relation to this world a limitless compassion drawing all beings toward *nirvāṇa*. This is the 'other story' to which Cook alludes in his last sentence.

But on the other hand, if we 'demythologize' that traditional Buddhist world-view, as it seems that Cook does, we are left with a Dharma which is good news for a few but exceedingly bad news for most of the human race. For enlightenment can only be attained in this present life, and in this present life it has always been the case that the vast majority of human beings do not attain it. (There are, for example, only two or three hundred Zen masters alive at any one time). It is of course true that, in principle, everyone is free to attain *nirvāṇa*. But this is an ironic truth, like the fact that in a desperately poor Third World country everyone is free to become a millionaire. The actual conditions of life are such that the great good of which the Dharma speaks is only for a very small spiritual élite. This is a chilly thought indeed; and I want to ask whether the Buddhist picture of our human situation as a whole is really as pessimistic as that? Is its implied account of the nature of things really such bad news for the generality of men and women, even though good news for a fortunate few? I can also put my question by asking how Cook integrates the story which he tells with the other story which he reserves for another time? Let us come to the time when both stories have been told and the full picture emerges.

19

Response to John Hick

Francis H. Cook

John Hick has raised two questions: where is the locus of the chilliness I have spoken of, and is the Buddhist teaching 'good news' for just a small number of dedicated Buddhists? I will try to be brief in my response.

The answer to the first question is easy, and I thought that I had made it clear in my response to Ives's chapter. My reference to the 'chilly and uncompromising' nature of Buddhist teachings was made within the context of the subject of discussion, the existence and nature of a religious ultimate. My point was that as I read the literature (and hence it is my own 'hard-nosed' reading), Buddhism does not incorporate within its structure the concept of a religious ultimate, including Buddha, *Dharma-kāya*, and *Nirvāṇa*. Nāgārjuna, at least, denies their ultimacy, whatever some of the non-Mahayana sects may have claimed then or slightly earlier. I interpret Buddhists like him to be saying that concepts such as 'the Ultimate' are just that, *concepts*, and do not have any real, objective referent. Hence, the concept of 'ultimate', however defined, must be rejected. There may indeed be a felt *need* among people for such an entity, but empirical evidence does not divulge any such entity, and it is at best unwise to base one's life on an assumption, and at worst it is counterproductive and harmful.

I spoke of empirical evidence. The *experience* of emptiness (and not the theory of or speculation concerning emptiness) reveals that everything without exception exists contingently as a function of other things, and the consequence of this is that everything becomes relativized. What can be ultimate? Emptiness? Emptiness is not any sort of thing which can be ultimate but is simply the manner in which things are what they are. I believe that this is the message of scriptural and commentarial literature, whatever may exist in the minds of believers. It is said to be the way things really are, assuming the status of a Law (Dharma), and this is what the Buddha

138

taught. As the scriptures say, that Law is eternal and omnipresent, whether or not Buddhas appear in the world to articulate it.

Thus, the chilliness is not in the minds of believers, who, on the contrary, do believe in ultimates and find many ways to warm up the Dharma. Most forms of Buddhism over the centuries have, on the other hand, based themselves pretty squarely on the teaching of emptiness which negates all ultimates, including the Ultimate. Buddhism has always realized that its teachings were uncompromising as far as human desires are concerned and has characterized itself as *pratiloma*, 'against the grain', rather than 'with the grain' (*anuloma*). But what other choice does any religion have than to proclaim what it understands to be the facts?

The issue of the availability or possibility of liberation certainly needs to be addressed, for Buddhism in most of its forms is demanding and difficult. Hick is concerned, for instance, that there are (he says) only about two hundred Zen masters in the whole world. I do not know how many there are, but this is really irrelevant, because Zen masters and enlightened beings are not necessarily the same thing. The choosing of successors in the Zen patriarchal lineage involves a number of factors, including teaching talent, and perhaps including personal preferences and politics. However, outside Zen itself, there are many Buddhists now living who have acquired some degree of enlightenment.

But the above remarks are all speculative and beside the point. The point is that Buddhism claims that enlightenment is in fact available to any and all who make the effort to have it. That few choose to make the effort is not a defect in Buddhism but must reflect the sedimented delusion and craving of beings who do not wish to know what is true and what not. That is the very *raison d'être* for Buddhism as a salvational scheme, to overcome delusion. The alternative would be for Buddhism to proclaim an easy, universal salvation based on a set of facts at complete variance with what it does proclaim to be the truth, but what would we think about such a religion? As I read Christian literature – Jesus, Paul, Luther and others – I find the same proclamation of what sounds like hard truth, universal sin and the absolute demand for faith. Presumably that faith is as available to all who want it as is Buddhist liberation, but I believe that the faith described by Luther (and Shinran in Pure Land Buddhism) is extremely difficult. I wonder how many Christians have achieved this faith over the centuries? Yet Christianity must proclaim what it believes to be the truth and cannot be otherwise than it is. It is not, therefore, a defect of Buddhism and Christianity that they paint a bleak picture of the human condition and demand hard choices and active seeking for deliverance. The defect is in the human heart, which puts its trust in idols, seeks the easy way, and wreathes itself in sentimentality and illusion. Both religions, I have come to believe, offer human beings a trust or assurance that guides them in life and helps them face the end, which are surely the basic functions of a religion. However, that trust is neither easy nor free. It comes only when the individual 'dies' and is restored to life free from fear. The good news is that anyone can win this trust; the bad news is that few make the effort.

Buddhism has not been unaware of the challenge it presents with its *pratiloma* approach. Pure Land Buddhism, for instance, offers an 'escape clause' for those who find other ways too difficult. The Buddha Amida has provided a realm beyond this world where enlightenment is easy and guaranteed, and Amida wills us, by imperial decree (*chokumei*), to be reborn there after death. This is the 'easy way' as contrasted with the 'difficult way' of such schools of Buddhism as Zen and Theravāda. Also, the so-called 'average' Buddhist in most cultures does not realistically expect to achieve enlightenment, which sounds remote, implausible, and perhaps undesirable ('enlightenment, yes, but not too soon, please'). Their Buddhism is that of merit-accumulation, in the hope of rebirth in a happy and fortunate form in the next life. This is a pleasant and comforting objective for millions of Buddhists who in effect reject the Buddhism of the scriptures and treatises with its austere world-view and its demands for meditation and other forms of committed engagement. Thus, in fact, Buddhism for most Buddhists is good news in exactly the sense implied in John Hick's question.

Part VI

20

The Real and Its Personae and Impersonae

John Hick

What do we mean by 'the Ultimate'? That beyond which there is nothing further. But then this could be simply the physical universe (including ourselves); there may be nothing more than it. However, the term 'the Ultimate' is useful mainly to signal the view that there *is* something more, something that transcends the physical universe, when the notion of A transcending B means not only that A is other than B but also that A is in some significant sense prior to, and/or more important or more valuable than, and/or explanatory of, B. I therefore propose to mean by the Ultimate that putative reality which transcends everything other than itself but is not transcended by anything other than itself. The Ultimate, so conceived, is related to the universe as its ground or creator, and to us human beings, as conscious parts of the Universe, as the source both of our existence and of the value or meaning of that existence.

This concept *may* be uninstantiated. It may be contingently uninstantiated, like the concept of a unicorn, or necessarily uninstantiated, like that of a square circle. But on the other hand it may not be like either of these. Notions of the Ultimate may be adequate or inadequate concepts – wholly or partly instantiated – of an all-important reality which transcends the physical Universe and our own psycho-physical selves. Whether such concepts are instantiatable, and if so instantiated, is of course the fundamental issue in the philosophy of religion. I have tried to address that basic question elsewhere. Acknowledging that it remains open, I propose nevertheless to discuss now a further question which arises for those who believe that there is or at least may be an ultimate reality which appropriately evokes human responses of the kind that we call religious.

The concept of the Ultimate to be outlined in this chapter differs in

143

an important respect from those discussed in the previous ones. Each of those concepts operates within a particular living religious tradition, entering into its distinctive mode of religious experience, shaping its liturgical language or meditative practice, and being reflectively described in its philosophy or theology. Each can thus be categorized as a primary religious concept, defining that (putative) reality transcending the worshipper or meditator upon which worship or meditation is focused. In contrast to this, the concept to be discussed here has been formed in the attempt to understand the relationship between those primary concepts. It functions within the philosophy of religion when this is not confined to the data of any one tradition but has a global scope. For it is the concept of the ground of this plurality of forms of religious experience and thought – the ultimate reality of which is variously conceived, experienced and responded to within the different traditions of the world.

It is the plurality of traditions that creates the problem which, as it seems to me, requires this concept for its resolution. If we can imagine there being only one religion in the world, and all religious persons thinking and experiencing in the same way, it would then be a natural and universal religious conviction that the Ultimate is as conceived in that tradition. But in fact, as we know, there are a number of religious histories each with its own concept or indeed family of concepts of the Ultimate. Hence the problem of the relationship between these and between the modes of religious experience which they inform. And the hypothesis that I want to consider here is that what they describe is not the Ultimate as it is in itself but as it is conceived in the variety of ways made possible by our varied human mentalities and cultures – our different modes of religious experience being in turn made possible by those concepts.

Such terms (in English) as the Real, the Ultimate, Ultimate Reality are commonly used to refer to this supposed *ne plus ultra*. None of them will suit everybody's linguistic taste. Accepting this I propose, arbitrarily, to speak of the Real, corresponding as it does to the Sanscrit *sat*, the Arabic *al Haq*, and the Chinese *shin*. And I shall be distinguishing between, on the one hand, the Real *an sich* – to use an expression which avoids the neuter as well as the feminine and the masculine – and on the other hand the Real as variously thought and experienced within the different religious traditions.

The paradigm of the Real *an sich* and its varied manifestations to human consciousness has to justify itself by its power to illuminate the history of religions. This offers significant pointers to it within each of the major traditions. Thus Christian thought has sometimes distinguished between God in God's eternal self-existent being, before or independently of creation, and God in relation to and thus as known by created beings – God *a se* and God *pro nobis*; Judaism, in its mystical Kabbalistic strand has distinguished between the infinite divine reality, *En Soph*, and the concrete God of the Bible; Islam, in its own mystical Sufi strand, has likewise distinguished between the ultimate reality, *al Haq*, and the Qur'anic Revealer to mankind; again Hindu advaitic thought distinguishes between *nirguna* Brāhman, beyond the scope of all human concepts, and *saguṇa* Brāhman, humanly known as Ishwara, the personal deity; and Buddhist thought, in the Mahāyāna, distinguishes between the eternal *dharma-kāya*, which is the ultimate and ineffable Buddha nature, and the *sambhoga-kāya* and *nirmāna-kāya*, in which that nature takes the form of individual Buddhas, some of whom become incarnate on this earth; and again, in recent Western thought, Paul Tillich has distinguished between God and the God above the God of theism,[1] and Gordon Kaufman between the real God and the available God.[2]

These distinctions were drawn for different purposes, each internal to its own tradition, and accordingly do not precisely coincide with the distinction that I want to draw. They do, however, suggest it to anyone who has the wider problem in mind. We can approach the distinction that we need through the familiar fact that even within a single theistic community of faith different individuals commonly operate with different mental pictures of God. If, for example, it were possible to inspect the images of God in the minds of a typical congregation of worshippers in a Christian church one Sunday morning, we should undoubtedly find wide variations. These images would range from the stern judge who sends misfortunes as punishments and whose presence inspires fear, to the gracious heavenly Father whose warm love envelops us; and would range in another dimension from God as an invisible person observing our every thought and act and prepared to intervene in answer to prayer in the smallest affairs of our lives, to God as 'high and lifted up' and 'inhabiting eternity', the maker and Lord of the universe, whose purposes are seen in the grand design of nature rather than in a detailed manipulation of events on earth. No doubt these images can be synthesized in a comprehensive theoretical definition. But the religious activities of worship, and the related forms of religious experience, involve limited images of God varying in their character and in the practical dispositions that they evoke. Nevertheless, it seems natural and indeed almost inevitable, from a Christian point of view, to say that Christians are all worshipping the same God, but each doing so through an image which focuses upon that aspect of the divine nature which is most relevant to their spiritual needs at the time. It is important to add that it is also possible for an image, at the extremes of the spectrum – for example, a Nazi image of God as the Lord of the Aryan race – to be so distorted that it cannot mediate a relationship with God as known in the central Christian tradition. But whilst our human images of the deity can thus be more adequate and less adequate, even the most adequate still require a distinction between God in the divine fullness and God as imaged in a variety of overlapping ways by different individuals and groups. And when we enlarge our field of vision to include the distinctively different but still overlapping concepts of God operating among Jews and Muslims, we shall naturally understand this wider range of differences in the same way though on a larger scale. For the three Peoples of the Book share a common biblical vision of the history of God's dealings with humanity. They manifestly intend to be worshipping the same, because the only, deity even though their mental images of that deity differ in the ways that separate the three traditions. For it is part of the distinctively Jewish self-understanding that the divine relationship to humanity is centred in God's dealings with the children of Israel; and part of the distinctively Christian self-understanding that God became incarnate as the founder of the Christian church; and part of the distinctively Muslim self-understanding that God has spoken finally and decisively in the Holy Qur'an. And so within each tradition it is believed that the other two Abrahamic faiths worship the same God through largely overlapping mental images of that God, whilst being, however, in each case mistaken at one key point. Each thus, whilst recognizing a common history, maintains its own unique centrality or sense of superiority.

There is, however, another possible interpretation of the situation, and one which does better justice to the apparently equal quality of worship and religious experience and of the fruits of this in human life within the three traditions. This is that their overlapping mental images of God are all produced by the impact of the divine Reality upon these three different streams of religious consciousness; but that the exclusivist interpretation which each tradition has put upon its own self-understanding is a human and limiting contribution. From this point of view God is authentically and savingly known to Jews in the Torah and the Rabbinic tradition; to Christians in the life and teachings of Jesus as mediated through the New Testament and the church; and to Muslims in the Qur'anic revelation through the prophet Muhammad. But in so far as Jews think of themselves as God's Chosen People in a sense which relegates all other peoples to an inferior relationship to God; and in so far as Christians think of Christianity as superior to all other religions because founded by God in person, with the implication that all human beings should become Christians; and in so far as Muslims think of the Qur'an as God's final revelation, superceding all others, with the implication that all human beings should become Muslims, they are each absolutizing their own human image of God in a way which denies the universal divine love and saving activity.

One way in which we can express the situation as we have thus far traced it is by saying that each stream of religious experience and thought has generated its own distinctive halo of self-validating mythology or self-enhancing metaphor – the mythologies of the Chosen People, of the uniquely incarnate God, and of God's definitive revelation to a particular people, the Arabs, in a particular human language. These are nevertheless true mythologies or true metaphors in so far as they evoke an appropriate response of devotion, in Jews to the Torah, in Christians to Christ, and in Muslims to the Qur'an. But none of these mythologies, nor the equivalent self-validating mythologies of other traditions, has universal validity, speaking to human beings as such; rather each is part of the history of a particular religio-cultural form of human life. And when we now take a yet larger view, and include the concepts of God operating within the Hindu tradition – Vishnu and Shiva, Kali and Durga, and the many other Gods and Goddesses of India – we find, at least among reflective worshippers, a general awareness that 'the Real (*sat*) is one, but sages name it variously'.[3] Accordingly Vaishnavites, whose devotional life is focused on the figure of Krishna as the saving incarnation of Vishnu, and Shaivites, with their devotional life focused on Shiva, do not dispute as to which of these is the true God; for they are conscious that both are authentic, though different and distinct, manifestations of the one ultimate reality of Brahman. The same is true within Mahayana Buddhism, in which Amida Buddha and Mahavairocana Buddha have been worshipped as the central Buddha by Pure Land and Esoteric Buddhists respectively for many centuries, but their difference in worship has led to no serious conflicts between them. This is simply because both Amida and Mahavairocana are regarded as different manifestations of one and the same *dharma-kāya* which is in reality empty, open and formless.[4]

Although the Indian and the Semitic deities lack a relationship to a common strand of human history, both groups function in the same way within the forms of life to which they belong. They should accordingly be interpreted on the same principle. Shiva and Krishna and Yahweh and Allah and the Heavenly Father, then, name different concrete images of the Real operating in the religious consciousness and life of different human communities. Each is thought of, experienced, and responded to as the Lord, the object of our devotion, the determiner of our destiny, the Ultimate in relation to us. And from a religious point of view we must say that each is indeed an authentic, life-giving manifestation of the Real within a different strand of human life. We thereby differ from the traditional formulations of faith, not in their affirmation of a transcendent divine Reality, but in the claim made within each tradition that it alone embodies the only fully valid and efficacious form of relationship to that Reality.

This position would seem to be in competition with three others. One is atheism: the Gods are all imaginary projections of the human mind. This is the naturalistic possibility which I noted but set aside at the beginning; for I am seeking here a *religious* interpretation of the phenomena of religion. A second possibility is religious exclusivism: our own God – whether we be Jew or Christian, Hindu or Muslim – exists, whilst the others are figments of human imagination. This possibility, however, is rendered implausible, in my view, by the fact that the effects in human life of devotion to these different Gods are so similar – both the good effect of the overcoming of self-centredness and the growth of love or compassion, and the bad effect of providing a validation of collective greed and aggression. If in one case the good is to be attributed to the influence of a real divine being and evil to human perversion, the same should be done in each case – unless there is some clear reason to the contrary; and the only reason offered is each tradition's conviction, in its more exclusivist moods, of its own unique superiority.

The third possibility is polytheism: the Gods are all real as ontologically distinct beings. One could, of course, apply this principle to all of the hundreds of thousands of deities known in the history of religion; but let us simplify our task here by restricting it to the Gods of the great monotheistic faiths. Yahweh or Adonai, then, is a real divine Person, and the Heavenly Father (or perhaps the Holy Trinity considered as a unity) is another real divine Person, and Allah is yet another real divine Person, and God as worshipped by the Sikhs is another, and Shiva yet another. . .

In commenting upon this possibility let me distinguish it from the hypothesis that I am advancing and show why the latter seems to me preferable. There is a sense in which, for example, the Yahweh of the Hebrew scriptures and the Krishna of the *Bhagavad Gita* are two different Gods. Yahweh is known only in his relationship to the Jewish people; he is a part of their history and they are a part of his. The universe of discourse which he inhabits is that of distinctively Jewish faith, and the strand of history in which he has operated runs through the Middle East and into the Jewish diaspora. Krishna on the other hand belongs to a different universe of religious discourse; and the strand of history within which he has revealed himself is that of ancient India. We have here two spheres of religious consciousness which do not at any point touch one another. Yahweh exists within and indeed as the centre of the Jewish world-view, and only a Jew can know Yahweh as his God. Krishna, on the other hand, exists within and at the centre of the quite different Vaishnavite Hindu world-view, and only a Hindu can know Krishna as his God. Thus far it looks as though there are here two autonomous language-games which should not be confused or mixed, even though they are indirectly related as distant members of the wide family of religious language-games. But nevertheless when we take note of them both in the same field of intellectual vision a problem becomes evident. Within the Hebrew world view Yahweh (or Adonai) is believed, as one of his essential attributes, to be the sole maker of heaven and earth,[5] and in the world-view of the *Bhagavad Gita* Krishna is believed to be the sole source of the universe.[6] If, then, we take the polytheistic view that Yahweh and Krishna both exist in some relatively straightforward sense, one (at most) can be what he has revealed himself to be, namely the creator or source of the universe, whilst the other must either be a deceiver or be deceived. Thus the worshippers either of Yahweh or Krishna must be worshipping a false god. And yet each is at the centre of an equally rich and spiritually sustaining religious life within which men and women are – and so far as we can tell are to an equal extent – brought to a self-giving love of God and to compassion towards their neighbours. The fruits of faith do not distinguish between the two Gods as respectively real and unreal, authentic and spurious. It therefore seems to me that the two viable options at this point are the naturalistic denial of both as figments of our imagination and the religious acceptance of both as authentic manifestations, or 'faces', or personae, or appearances to human consciousness, of the Real *an sich*.

Let me now adopt one of these terms and develop a little the idea of a plurality of divine personae. By a human persona I mean a public mask or social role which has developed in one's interaction with others and which has its existence within the ongoing process of a system of personal relationships. A permanently solitary consciousness – if we can imagine one – would have no persona since it would not exist in relationship to other consciousnesses. Personality, in distinction from consciousness as such, is essentially interpersonal, and presupposes a common world within which social life can take place. Accordingly the various divine personae, Yahweh and Krishna and Durga and Allah and Shiva and the Heavenly Father (or the Father, Son and Holy Ghost), and so on, have been formed in the interaction between the Real and different human religio-cultural communities. They exist at the interface between the Real and the various streams of historical consciousness. Thus the Yahweh persona has come about and developed in the impact of the Real upon the distinctively Hebraic consciousness of the Jewish people through the centuries; whilst the Krishna persona has come about in the impact of the Real upon distinctively Indian consciousness within the Vaishnavite tradition. And the reason why the Real is so preponderantly thought and experienced as personal in the history of religions is presumably that as persons we need, in our relationship with the Real, a personal cosmic presence to address and to be addressed by. Accordingly the different divine personae have formed as manifestations of the Real, in relation to the different streams of human consciousness. They are the Real as known, necessarily in human terms, within this or that religious tradition.

Can this paradigm of the Real becoming manifest in different ways, which have been partly formed by the human contribution to awareness of them, be applied also to the thought and experience of the non-theistic traditions – advaitic Hinduism and most of Buddhism? I have suggested that the Real as perceived through one set of religio-cultural 'lenses' appears as a range of personal deities, which are the personae of the Real. Can we also say that the Real as perceived through another set of religio-cultural 'lenses' appears as a range of non-personal absolutes, which are the impersonae of the Real?

I believe that we can; though only after two obstacles have been surmounted.

The first obstacle is the question whether what is experienced in non-theistic mysticism is indeed believed to be the Ultimate. So far as Hindu mysticism is concerned the answer is non-controversially Yes: Brahman is thought of as the Ultimate Reality. But what of Buddhism? Here we must remember that there is (as in the case of the other great traditions) not simply Buddhism in the singular but Buddhisms in the plural. The full range of meditational practices and philosophical interpretations inspired by the Buddha covers territory on both sides of the border between what I shall call the naturalistic or humanist, and the supranaturalistic or religious, types of world-view. As I am using the terms, humanism or natural-ism does not require a concept of the Ultimate; whereas religious, or supranaturalistic, world-views do – each religious tradition having its own distinctive variation. There is, then, a humanist form of Buddhism which consists essentially in the practice of meditation without any associated supranatural beliefs. The fruit of meditation in the purification of the mind from the corrosions of ego-anxiety, and a consequent non-judgmental acceptance of this transitory world of which we are part, is an end in itself. The trappings of zazen drawn from Japanese monastic life – the meditation hall, the discipline, the drums and chants – are accepted as helpful aids to meditation; and such traditional Buddhist ideas as innumerable rebirths, the heavens and hells, the gods and bodhisattvas, are demythologized and regarded as popular aids to the imagination. All this is within the humanistic or naturalistic assumption that we are simply fleeting moments of consciousness, here one moment and gone the next, within the continuously transforming field of energy which is the physical Universe.

I fully accept that Buddhism permits this kind of humanistic development; and indeed it is this that constitutes much of its attraction to many Western minds reacting against simplistically literal understandings of theism. (See, for example, Don Cupitt's *Taking Leave of God*, 1980, and subsequent writings.) However, I question whether the main streams of Buddhist thought have understood themselves in this way.

In the Pali scriptures of the Thervada, *nirvāna* (*nibbana*) is certainly sometimes presented in purely negative terms as simply the cessation of the grasping self and its attendant anxieties. It is the 'blowing out' of the ego with its inevitable sorrows. But there is also in the tradition a strong element of positive and indeed supranaturalistic teaching about *nirvāna*. Thus the Buddha declares, in a famous passage, 'Monks, there is a not-born, a not-become, a not-made, a not-compounded. Monks, if that unborn, not-become, not-made, not-compounded were not, there would be apparent no escape from this here that is born, become, made, compounded'.[7] Again, in the *Majjhima-Nikaya nirvāna* is described as 'the unborn . . unaging . . undecaying . . undying . . unsorrowing . . stainless',[8] and in the *Samyutta-Nikaya* as 'the further shore . . the unfading . . the stable . . the invisible . . the taintless . . the peace . . the deathless . . the excellent . . the blissful . . the security . . the wonderful . . the marvellous . . the free from ill . . the island . . the cave of shelter . . the stronghold . . the refuge . . the goal'.[9] This sounds more like supranaturalistic-religious than naturalistic-humanist language. And it is, I think, so understood by most of the leading Theravadins of today; for example, Narada Thera, in his commentary of *The Dhammapada*, speaks of *nirvāna* as 'the permanent, immortal, supra-mundane state which cannot be expressed in mundane terms'.[10]

This positive use of the concept of *nirvāna*, as pointing to the ultimate ineffable reality with which religion is concerned, was further developed within the Mahāyāna. Edward Conze sum-marizes, 'The ultimate reality, also called Dharma by the Buddhists, or Nirvana, is defined as that which stands completely outside the sensory world of illusion and ignorance, a world inextricably inter-woven with craving and greed. To get somehow to that reality is the supremely worthwhile goal of the Buddhist life. The Buddhist idea of ultimate reality is very much akin to the philosophical notion of the 'Absolute', and not easily distinguished from the notion of God among the more mystical theologians, like Dionysius Areopagita and Eckart'.[11] And when we turn to Zen, which is the strand of Buddhism that is most readily open to a purely humanistic in-terpretation, we find members of the very influential Kyoto school speaking of religion as 'man's search for true reality', indeed for the 'Great Reality' (Keiji Nishitani),[12] and saying that 'nirvana is nothing but Ultimate Reality' (Masao Abe).[13] They emphasize that the characterization of Reality as *śūnyatā* (Emptiness, Void, Nothing-ness) is a way of expressing a transcendence of all human thought-forms. As D. T. Suzuki wrote, 'To say that reality is 'empty' means that it goes beyond definability, and cannot be qualified as this or that'. Again, '*Dharmakāya* or *prajñā*, being "emptiness" itself and having no tangible bodily existence, has to embody itself in a form and be *manifested* as a stalk of bamboo, as a mass of foliage, as a fish, as a man, as a Bodhisattva, as a mind, and so forth. But these manifestations themselves *are* not the *Dharmakāya* or *prajñā*, which is more than forms or ideas or modes of existence'.[14]

Thus it seems that there is deeply embedded in the Buddhist tradition the belief in an ultimate Reality, the eternal *dharmakāya* or Buddha nature, also characterized as *śūnyatā*, with which a right relationship, unitive or communitive, is attained in the final experience of enlightenment.

But what of the distinctive Mahayana discovery, central to Zen, that *nirvāna* and *samsāra* are one? What is discovered is a way of experiencing the world as it is, in its pure 'suchness'. This 'suchness', or as-it-is-ness, is also its 'emptiness' of any substantiality or permanence, and this 'emptiness' is, paradoxically, fullness of 'wondrous being'[15] in the ever new reality of the present moment. This depth of reality is experienced by transcending the normal ego point of view, in which everything is perceived as it affects the self, and seeing things as they are for their own sake in their presentational immediacy. Like other modes of Buddhist experience this can be interpreted, or contextualized, both religiously and humanistically. For Zen-humanism the experience of the world in its full wonder and beauty is an end in itself, devoid of any implications concerning the structure of the Universe beyond the evident fact that its incessant flow includes this present moment of experience. Religious Zen, on the other hand, also finds in this experience of the world a clue to the nature of reality, transcending our own individual experience, as to be rejoiced in because it offers the bliss of *nirvāna* to all conscious beings. Such an affirmation of the good in the sense of the to-be-rejoiced-in character of reality as a whole – not just good for a fortunate few but eventually for all – is of the essence of religion. For if the goodness thus affirmed is secure and reliable it cannot be a mere chance moment waiting to be dissolved again in a structureless flow of change. It must, in other words, have an ultimate character. To affirm the goodness of the universe – which William James, in my view rightly, identified as the essential message of religion[16] – is to affirm an ultimate reality transcending the flux of change and chance, a reality which is in its relation to us to be rejoiced in. And in the Buddhist tradition this eternal reality is variously known as *nirvāna*, the *dharma-kāya*, *śūnyatā*.

Thus it seems to me that our hypothesis, in its application to the non-theistic traditions, is able to surmount this first obstacle: in Hinduism and Buddhism there is an affirmation of the Ultimate either as the infinite consciousness of Brahman or as the ultimate character of reality which is from our point of view good.

The second obstacle arises from a general difference between the traditions of Semitic and of Indian origin. If by the mystical we mean, as I think we should mean, simply the top end of the scale of intensity within the experiential element in religion, then mysticism plays a much more central role in the Eastern than in the Western traditions. Hinduism centres upon human consciousness, in all its emotional, volitional, intellectual and intuitive modes, and offers a transition from the anxiety-ridden delusion of *maya* to the blissful self-consciousness of the *ātman*, which is one with Brahman, the Ultimate itself. Buddhism likewise centres upon our present consciousness, suffering from the anguished fears and worries generated by the self-concerned ego. For the ego is attached by a thousand bonds of grasping desire and fearful avoidance to a world that it cannot control, so that the ever-changing stream of life, involving the ineluctable possibilities of sickness, poverty, shame, injustice, and the inevitabilities of old age, decay and death, are felt as a perpetual threat. All this is the *dukkha* from which we can be liberated only by transcending the self-centred point of view and entering into the egoless state of *nirvāna*. Thus, for both Hindu and Buddhist traditions right experiencing is an end in itself, whilst right believing has a subsidiary and instrumental value in pointing out the way to liberation.

For Judaism, Christianity and Islam, on the other hand, experience has generally been secondary to right belief or right behaviour. In Christianity right belief has been given a primary place, so that those who harbour 'wrong beliefs' have had to be cast out of the church as heretics – and *extra ecclesiam nulla salus*! In Judaism participation in the ritual life of the people through the centuries has generally been regarded as more important than the holding of correct beliefs; orthopraxy has had priority over orthodoxy. In Islam certain basic beliefs – above all in the uniqueness and absoluteness of God and in God's revelation through the Prophet – have been seen as essential; but beyond this the stress has been upon the activities of prayer, fasting, alms-giving, pilgrimage and the organization of life in an Islamic pattern. Of course, there are profound mystical strands within each of these traditions of Semitic origin. But, historically, those strands have had a marginal place and have not infrequently been objects of suspicion or even hostility on the part of the orthodox.

Now mysticism, such as is central to the non-theistic strands within Hinduism and Buddhism, reports a direct, unmediated, often unitive, awareness of the Ultimate. The subject-object relationship is said to be transcended. There is no longer any epistemic distance between the human consciousness and the Ultimate itself, and accordingly no scope for a human activity of interpretation. Thus according to *advaita* Vedanta liberation involves the experience of oneness with Brahman; and according to Buddhism the attainment of *nirvāna* is the experience of one's eternal Buddha nature, or (in Zen) of the ever-changing world, no longer seen in the distorting perspective of the ego, but experienced now as itself *nirvāna*. But such a unitive and unmediated experience of the Ultimate does not fit the model that we have adopted for the theistic forms of religious experience, namely a reality, itself beyond the scope of human thought and experience, being mediately known in different ways from within the different religio-cultural streams of life. Thus far, then, it would seem that the model will apply to the theistic but not to the non-theistic religions.

However, recent epistemological discussions of mysticism have suggested that an interpretative element is always and unavoidably present even in the ostensibly unitive experience. For the mystic is still an embodied human mind; and this always functions in accordance with its own inherent structure, its cultural formation and individual experience. And there is considerable evidence that a person who has been spiritually trained by an *advaitic* guru, whose mind has been steeped in the Vedas and Upanishads and the writings of Shankara, and who has for years practised a form of *advaitic* yoga, will have a characteristically different experience of the Ultimate from one who has been spiritually trained by a Zen master, whose mind is steeped in Zen literature, and who has practised zazen for years in a monastery or meditation centre. The one will have a distinctively *advaitic* experience of the Ultimate as Brahman, the other a distinctively Zen experience of the Ultimate as the pure 'suchness' of everything seen as 'wondrous being', devoid of all ego-distortion. The strong correlation of the type of experience with the spiritual practice and its associated philosophy unmistakably indicates that the two minds bring their Vedantic or Zen ideas and modes of apperception with them into their mystical experiencing, determining the form that it takes.

It therefore seems to me that the second hurdle can also be surmounted. There does seem to be in the non-theistic forms of religious experience a culturally variable human contribution paralleling the culturally variable contribution to the different kinds of theistic experience.

There are, then, according to the hypothesis I am outlining, a plurality of impersonae as well as of personae of the Real. None of these is the Real *an sich*; but each of them is the Real as it affects a particular stream of religious consciousness. In Kantian terms, the noumenal Real is experienced – that is, enters into the phenomenal or experiencable realm – through one or other of two basic concepts – the concept of deity, or of the Real as personal, and the concept of the absolute, or of the Real as non-personal. (The term 'absolute' seems to be the nearest we have, although it is by no means ideal, being less congenial to Buddhist than to Hindu thinking.) However, we do not experience deity or the absolute in general. The human mind is always conscious of either in a specific way and as having a particular character. And because there are many consolidated historical forms of human mentality, reflecting the different ways of being human that have developed over the millennia, the history of religions shows a corresponding range of divine personae and of metaphysical impersonae.

What can we say about the Real *an sich*? Only that it is the ultimate reality that we postulate as the ground of the different forms of religious experience and thought in so far as they are more than human projection. To affirm the Real is to affirm that religious belief and experience in its plurality of forms is not simply delusion but constitutes our human, and therefore imperfect, partial and distorted range of ways of being affected by the universal 'presence' of the Real. But we cannot apply to the noumenal Real any of the distinctions with which we structure our phenomenal, including our religious, experience. We cannot say that it is personal or impersonal, one or many, active or passive, substance or process, good or evil, just or unjust, purposive or purposeless. No such categories can be applied, either positively or negatively, to the noumenal. Thus, whilst it is not correct to say, for example, that the Real is personal, it is also not correct to say that it is impersonal – nor that it is both personal and impersonal, or neither personal nor impersonal. All that one can say is that these concepts, which have their use in relation to human experience, do not apply, even analogically, to the Real *an sich*.

Thus the Real *an sich* cannot be the object of a religious cult. We cannot worship it or achieve union with it. We worship one or other of its personae, or we seek union with one or other of its impersonae. And in so far as a deity or an absolute is an authentic manifestation of the Real, promoting the transformation of human existence from self-centredness to Reality-centredness, the form of worship or of meditation focused upon him or her or it constitutes 'true religion'. In principle we are free to choose between the personal and non-personal manifestations of the Real; and among the personae, to choose which God or Goddess, or group of deities, to worship; and again, among the impersonae, to choose to mediate towards the realization of Brahman or of Nirvana. In practice, a small minority do so choose; and it may be that that minority is becoming bigger. But for the large majority of us it has always been the case that the choice is in effect made by birth and upbringing.

What I have been outlining is a theory or hypothesis, a possible framework for thought concerning the religious life of humanity. What use might such an hypothesis have?

(1) It may satisfy our intuition that each of the great world faiths has such value that it is false and harmful to regard any one of them alone as true or authentic and the others as false or inauthentic. The hypothesis spells out to some extent the insight expressed by the Muslim mystic Jalālaldîn Rūmî, 'The lamps are different, but the Light is the same'.[17]

(2) At the same time, however, the hypothesis can remove any temptation to think of the different traditions as 'all the same' or 'all alike', and can free us to notice and to be fascinated by all the differences that the phenomenology of religion reveals.

(3) The hypothesis may thus provide a framework for inter-faith dialogue, and an explicit basis for the hope that each tradition may learn from and be changed by its encounter with the others. For if each represents a different human perspective on the Real, each may be able to enlarge its own vision by trying to look through the lenses that others have developed.

Notes

1. Paul Tillich, *The Courage to Be* (Yale University Press, 1952) p. 190.
2. Gordon Kaufman, *God the Problem* (Harvard University Press, 1972) p. 86.
3. *Rig Veda*, I, 164, 46.
4. Masao Abe, 'A Dynamic Unity in Religious Pluralism', in John Hick and Hasan Askari (eds), *The Experience of Religious Diversity* (London: Gower, 1985) pp. 178–9.
5. Genesis 1:1.
6. *Bhagavad Gita* 9, 4.
7. Udana, 80.
8. *Majjhima-Nikaya*, I, 163. *The Middle Length Sayings*, trans. I. B. Horner, Vol. I, pp. 206–7.
9. *Samyutta-Nikaya*, IV, 369–71. *The Kindred Sayings*, trans. C. A. F. Rhys Davids, Part IV, pp. 261–3.
10. Narada Thera, *The Dhammapada*, 2nd ed. Colombo: Vajirarama, 1972, pp. 24–5.
11. Edward Conze, *Buddhism, Its Essence and Development* (New York: Harper Torchbooks, 1975) pp. 110–11.
12. Keiji Nishitani, *Religion and Nothingness*, trans. Jan Van Bragt (Berkeley: University of California Press, 1982) pp. 6 and 20.
13. Masao Abe, 'God, Emptiness, and the True Self', in *The Buddha Eye*, ed. Frederick Frank (New York: Crossroads, 1982) p. 65.
14. D. T. Suzuki, 'The Buddhist Conception of Reality', *The Buddha Eye*, *op. cit.*, pp. 103 and 97.
15. 'True Emptiness is Wondrous Being', *Mōjingengenkan*.
16. William James, *The Varieties of Religious Experience*, beginning of Lecture XX.
17. 'The One True Light', trans. R. A. Nicholson in *Rūmî: Poet and Mystic* (London and Boston: Mandala Books, 1978) p. 166.

21

Reply: Can John Hick Say What He Said?

John K. Roth

It has been a while since I opened my worn copy of Ludwig Wittgenstein's *Tractatus Logico-Philosophicus*. Writing this response to John Hick's last chapter made me turn to it again because I needed to quote correctly the book's last line: 'What we cannot speak about we must pass over in silence'.

Can John Hick say what he said in his chapter on 'The Real and Its Personae and Impersonae'? Well, he wrote the chapter; thus, in some sense the answer to the title-question of this response must be *yes*. That affirmative answer nevertheless fails to satisfy me. I am left feeling that *no* is the better reply. Let me say why. In doing so, I shall also attempt to raise some other issues that lurk in the pages of his essay.

To get at the heart of the matter, we must go to the end of Professor Hick's exposition. Before settling there, however, recall what the discussion is all about. John Hick finds the plurality of religious traditions creating a problem that needs resolution. The problem emerges, he says, because 'there are a number of religious histories each with its own concept or indeed family of concepts of the Ultimate'. Each tradition, moreover, has tendencies that put an 'exclusivist interpretation . . . upon its own self-understanding'. The task therefore is to see whether there is a way to explain and justify the varieties of religious experience while simultaneously defusing the conflict among them by showing their exclusivist and absolutizing tendencies to be without warrant.

Both aims are laudable – the first because, as Hick argues, its fulfillment might 'satisfy our intuition that each of the great world faiths has . . . value'; the second because today's world can use just about any reduction of conflict it can get. So far so good, but the waters muddy as Hick advances these aims by putting what is essentially an old hypothesis in some attire that appears new but in fact is not.

Central to Hick's analysis is the idea that no religious tradition describes 'the Ultimate as it is in itself'. Rather each involves an interpretation of what Hick prefers to call 'the Real *an sich*'. These interpretations reflect finite human mentalities and historic-cultural locations. According to Hick, they provide 'the Real as variously thought and experienced within the different religious traditions'. To support his hypothesis about 'the Real *an sich*', Hick thinks he must bridge a gap between religious perspectives that regard the Ultimate as somehow personal and those that say otherwise. We shall come back to that problem shortly, but with this much set forth, we can focus on the end, the part of Hick's paper where Wittgenstein's conclusion – 'What we cannot speak about we must pass over in silence' – comes to bear.

By making his distinction between 'the Real *an sich*' or 'the noumenal Real' on the one hand and 'the Real as variously thought and experienced within the different religious traditions' on the other, Hick has chosen to enter a Kantian labyrinth. There, more questions have usually been unanswered than resolved, and Hick's case is no exception to that rule. The entry to the Kantian labyrinth attracts Hick understandably because within is the assurance – should we say an *absolutist* assurance? – that no particular religious tradition could legitimately claim to have an exclusivist hold on divine truth. Hick underwrites this assurance with a vengeance. In sum, he says, 'we cannot apply to the noumenal Real any of the distinctions with which we structure our phenomenal, including our religious, experience'.

That's the sentence that brought Wittgenstein to mind. One thing 'the Real' involves *is* a distinction; and, as Hick uses 'the Real *an sich*', he uses it precisely to structure 'our phenomenal, including our religious, experience'. Ironically, however, in his eagerness to prevent exclusiveness and absolutism, Hick saws off the limb on which he is trying to sit. That claim is true, I believe, because in his speaking about 'the Real *an sich*' Hick is doing the very thing that his own epistemology rules out.

This problem is not new. But why Hick gets cut off by it is puzzling, because the history of philosophy indicates that even Kant never fully satisfied those who kept questioning how his epistemology enabled him to speak of 'things in themselves'. Perhaps such reality is a necessary condition to account for experience as it actually occurs. But that Kantian move did not convince everyone. In the case at hand in our present discussion, Hick's Kantianism is even less persuasive because he admits that 'the Real *an sich*' is not even a necessary condition for religious experience as we know it. The concept, he is at pains to suggest, may well be uninstantiated, assuming that it can be a meaningful concept at all under the terms of his own religious epistemology.

The whole enterprise of this paper hinges on whether we can say *yes* or should say *no* to the question 'Can John Hick say what he said?' His particular Kantian approach, I suggest, makes the latter outcome most likely. Thus, Hick might well take Wittgenstein's counsel to heart – 'What we cannot speak about we must pass over in silence' – or else resist the temptations that lure him into the Kantian labyrinth but do not liberate him from it.

Whatever the fundamental approach, however, this paper contains other difficulties that its author needs to address. For example, Hick tries valiantly to show that 'the Real *an sich*' can harmoniously encompass historical religious traditions that affirm ultimate reality to be personal and those that do not. His higher synthesis rests in large measure on a belief that all the great religions say essentially the same thing. Specifically, for instance, the essence of all religion involves what Hick calls 'an affirmation of the good in the sense of the to-be-rejoiced-in character of reality as a whole'.

That position does not assuage my scepticism, for at this point I am reminded not of Wittgenstein but of someone very different, namely Abraham Lincoln, who once made a point that fits aptly here. In the middle of the American Civil War – and I think the circumstances are not irrelevant for our purposes – Lincoln observed that 'we all declare for liberty; but in using the same *word* we do not all mean the same *thing*'. As the varieties of religious experience employ the terms, 'goodness' and 'joy' may have family resemblances, but their meanings are not identical, probably not even essentially. To suggest that the gap between the ultimacy of personhood and its absence can be bridged by some general affirmation of the goodness of the Universe does more to beg the question than to resolve the dilemma at hand.

Parenthetically I might add that the vagueness at this juncture in Hick's account is all the more surprising because in studying his criticisms of other authors (for example, in a recent book, *Encountering Jesus*, edited by Stephen T. Davis), Professor Hick often plays the role of identifying 'soft' concepts and prodding their authors to say clearly and concretely what they mean. The tough-minded *persona* of the real John Hick, I believe, could help the more tender-minded *persona* who defends 'the Real *an sich*'.

The hypothesis that needs greater consideration than John Hick has given it is that his own hypothesis about 'the Real *an sich*' just won't work epistemologically or religiously. In that case we may be back where we were before: namely, with a variety of religious experiences that are irreducibly pluralistic, historically if not ultimately. Some of these may persist in exclusivist and absolutist ways as well. If that is where things come out when Hick's neo-Kantianism falls short, what are we to do?

I don't know the answer to that question, but John Hick's chapter leads me to make one suggestion that might merit some discussion. Whenever religion's expressions are exclusivist and/or absolutist, the liabilities attached to religious pluralism are intensified just to the degree that those exclusivist-absolutist expressions are wedded with political power. Inter-faith dialogue should be encouraged, no doubt; and we definitely need to keep enlarging our religious visions by trying, as John Hick says, 'to look through lenses that others have developed'. But even more important may be the task of exploring *how* religion and politics mix and mingle – which they always seem to do – and, in particular, how it may be the political factors more than the religious that make the exclusivist and absolutist tendencies of religion so dangerous. It is always possible for religious people – exclusivist or not – to disagree without attacking and killing each other. But it is harder to keep that from happening when religion is *charged* with politics. These are matters about which philosophers of religion ought not to keep silent, even if they must do so before 'the Real'.

To sum up my comments on John Hick's exposition, then, I would ask him to consider further three questions: (1) Strictly speaking, does Hick's epistemology permit him to say anything meaningful about 'the Real *an sich*'? (2) Can the gap between religions that stress the personal and those that do not really be bridged by appeals to generalities such as a shared affirmation of the goodness of the Universe, and, if not, where are we left? (3) If we are left with religious pluralism that is irreducible and even destined to remain laced with absolutism and exclusivism, are the attendant problems, in the final practical analysis, primarily religious or political? On all of these points my hope is that John Hick will not hand back Wittgenstein – 'What we cannot speak about we must pass over in silence' – but will instead show us that what John Hick says he can say indeed.

22

Comment on John Hick

Stephen T. Davis

Hick's recent work on this topic is a bold attempt to solve a thorny theological problem. Here are the three reasons I am unconvinced.

(1) I question the evidence for the theory. Why hold that various views of the ultimate are phenomenal apprehensions of one noumenon? The theory may work *vis–à-vis* the God of Judaism and the God of Christianity, since Christians hold that their God is the same as the Jews' God. Perhaps the theory also works *vis-à-vis* this God and the God of Islam, since their properties turn out to be remarkably similar. But when we compare Yahweh with, say, the 'voidness' spoken of in Mahayana Buddhism, the notions are far too different; the claim that they are noumenally identical seems absurd. The *only* evidence in the theory's favour is a strong desire that it be true in relation to the envisioned alternatives, exclusivism or atheism.

(2) I am dubious about Hick's use of the Kantian distinction between *noumenon* and *phenomenon*. If 'the Real', that is, the religious noumenon, is (as Hick says) 'beyond the scope of human thought and experience', then I am puzzled by the many human concepts (for instance, *ground, beyond, real, explain, one*) Hick applies to it in his various writings. This at least requires explanation. For example, how does Hick know that there is but one noumenal ground of our many apprehensions of the ultimate? His answer, I suppose, would be that since the behavioural effect in the various religions is roughly the same, there is no reason to postulate more than one ground. But surely the behavioural effect is not the same – Jews, for example, behave very differently as Jews than Zen Buddhists do as Zen Buddhists. But, more importantly, is this not to do exactly what Hick forbids us to do, viz., apply a human concept ('one') to the Real? Another example: how does Hick know (what I have heard him say) that bad aspects of the religions come from purely human elements in them (with the implication that the Real is the ground of only the good elements)?

(3) Suppose that x and y disagree about the ultimate. How are we to interpret such a situation? Clearly there are only three possibilities:

1. x is right and y wrong;
2. y is right and x wrong;
3. Both are wrong.

It is important to see that Hick advocates option 3. All the religions are mistaken in what they say about the Ultimate. Hick simply rejects the way most religions understand themselves (to the extent that they make truth claims about the Ultimate). In effect, then, Hick is calling for a liberal theological revolution in the religions. It is true that many traditions have a built-in scepticism about their own claims; nevertheless, adherents of the various religions almost always think their own statements about the Ultimate are closer to the truth than other statements. And this is just what Hick's theory no longer allows them to hold. Thus I suspect Hick's call will not be widely heeded – especially not in a time of resurgent fundamentalism in religions like Judaism, Christianity, Islam and Hinduism.

23

Comment on John Hick

John B. Cobb, Jr.

Hick's project is to find a way of understanding the several religious traditions so that their respective claims will not be in conflict. The ideal would be that believers in one tradition who understand themselves in the way he proposes could accept believers in other traditions as having equal, or at least comparable, claims to truth and validity. This is a worthy goal, one that I share. But I fear that the way in which Hick seeks to accomplish his purposes pays too high a price.

Hick seems to believe that full mutual acceptance hinges on the belief that all are related to the same Real which manifests itself to them in diverse ways. Among the several manifestations, personal and impersonal, questions of truth and error, superiority and inferiority, do not arise. This certainly is a gain in comparison with much of what we have inherited from the past.

But does this project succeed? One way of understanding it would be to hold that what he calls the Real is what Hindus have called *Nirguna Brahman* and Mahayana Buddhists have called *Dharmakaya*. Hindus and Buddhists know that *Brahman* and *Dharmakaya* manifest themselves in many ways and that believers usually relate themselves to this Real through the manifestations.

But Hick does not mean this, since to do so would be to adopt the view of some religious traditions against others, namely, that the Formless is Ultimate Reality and can be realized as such, whereas theists relate themselves to one of its manifestations as if that were Ultimate Reality itself. Hick, in contrast, seeks to be neutral as between *Nirguna Brahman* and Allah, to take examples from the two sides. Hence he calls *Nirguna Brahman* one manifestation of the Real, denying that it is a name for the Real as such. Allah is just as directly a manifestation of the Real, in Hick's view, as is *Nirguna Brahman*.

The problem is that to take this position is flatly to contradict the Vedantist idea of *Nirguna Brahman*. Of course, Hick is at liberty to argue with adherents of any and every tradition. But this must be a difficult argument. If the Vedantists tell Hick that what he names the Real is what they name *Nirguna Brahman*, how can Hick insist that *Nirguna Brahman* is a name for one among other manifestations of the Real? This seems both arbitrary and rude. In any case, it means that one can attain the irenic goal Hick pursues only by rejecting one of the deepest intuitions of a great religious tradition. That is a high price to pay!

Hick is forced to pay this price in order to be even-handed among the traditions. But it is questionable that theists will be happier to accept his interpretation of their faith than that of Vedantists. Of course, it is true that every idea or image of deity that has ever been present in a human mind is, as Hick says, the product of the impression of the Real upon historically and culturally conditioned human minds. This must be true of every way Allah has been conceived. But to believers in Allah, the fact that their images and meanings are distinct from the Real does not mean that Allah is distinct from the Real. The intention of believers in Allah is to name the Real in this way and thereby make certain claims about the nature of the Real and its way of being related to the world. To say that not only their ideas of Allah but also Allah as such is an appearance or manifestation of something else, namely, the Real, is not significantly different from asserting that Allah is a manifestation of *Nirguna Brahman*.

Now Hick may reply that since absolutist claims are so widespread in all the traditions there is no other way to overcome mutual prejudices than by the abandonment of the central conviction of each tradition. Earlier he asked Christians to give up Christocentrism for the sake of attaining a fuller acceptance of other religious traditions. Now he asks us to give up theocentrism as well. I for one am not interested in either move. I do not believe Hindus and Buddhists will be any more willing to give up what is central to their understanding and practice. I hope they will not. Would it not, for the sake of mutual appreciation, be better to affirm the deepest convictions of all rather than to negate them all?

24
Comment on John Hick

Christopher Ives

In his paper, John Hick draws a distinction between what he terms 'naturalistic or humanist' and 'supernaturalistic or religious' world-views in Buddhism. He argues that a 'religious' world-view includes a concept of the Ultimate as 'something more, something that transcends the physical universe'. In his paradigm of religious experience, this Ultimate is a noumenal Reality experienced phenomenally in different religious contexts.

From the present writer's perspective, actual Zen falls between the two world-views articulated by Hick, and, more importantly, the 'ultimate' and epistemology of Zen do not clearly fit Hick's paradigm. As Hick points out, Nishitani, Abe and other Zen philosophers argue that *śūnyatā*, the Mahayana Buddhist ultimate, transcends 'all human thought-forms', but this transcendence does not indicate that the Zen ultimate is some *thing* ('something') which transcends the physical Universe. For Zen, the Universe – physical *and* mental – lacks any unchanging essence or eternal being, and each thing is devoid (empty, *śūnya*) of independent existence. Hence, *śūnyatā* is ultimate in that it universally characterizes the nature of reality, the interconnected process of becoming. Though this may be regarded as lacking in 'religious' character, as a 'humanistic or naturalist assumption that we are simply fleeting moments of consciousness, here one moment and gone the next, within the continuously transforming field of energy which is the physical Universe', profound religious significance emerges in the existential and epistemological shift through which we realize this 'empty' nature of reality and rid ourselves of the attempt to reify ourselves or to find an unchanging, transcendent ultimate.

In this realization, one does not experience an ultimate object or noumenal Real as a phenomenon. The content of Zen religious experience is the actual world or objects in it. What *is* ultimate is the shift in our mode of experiencing, from self-centredness to reality-centredness (not Reality-centredness), from dualistic ego-subjectivity to liberated, 'emptied' subjectivity in which the split between the 'subject' and 'object', me and the content of experience, is overcome. This has crucial religious significance, even though it does not necessarily involve a 'supranatural' object of experience. That is to say, this shift is existentially salvific and conduces to the attributes and moral fruits (love and compassion) usually generated in what Hick deems genuine religious transformation.

Accordingly, 'naturalistic' statements in Zen should not be taken as lacking in 'religious' significance, nor should 'supranaturalistic' expressions like 'true reality' be taken as indicating a substantial, noumenal Real. (Indeed, it is precisely the reification of such expressions and concepts that the doctrine of *śūnyatā* denies.) In the words of Shin'ichi Hisamatsu, Zen may be deemed 'True-Humanism', a standpoint beyond naturalistic humanism and heteronomous supranaturalism.

25

Response to John Hick

Joseph Prabhu

I am impressed by the seriousness and depth of Hick's concern with the question of truth in the face of the different, and at times apparently conflicting, truth claims of the great world religions. On the one hand, he takes seriously the idea that the conceptions of the Ultimate embodied in these faiths are different but can still lay some claim to truth. On the other hand, precisely because he takes the question of truth seriously, he does not lapse into an easy and self-defeating relativism. He therefore offers a hypothesis that 'there are a plurality of impersonae as well as personae of the Real. None of these is Real *an sich*; but each of them is the Real as it affects a particular stream of religious consciousness'. I have a number of difficulties with this suggestion, which I shall state in very summary form.

(1) However much he claims that he is borrowing the noumenal/phenomenal distinction from Kant for his own conceptual purposes, which do not require a commitment to Kant's theoretical scheme, Hick enmeshes himself in difficulties similar to those which bedevil Kant's project. He wishes to make the Real a postulate, which in Kant's terminology can be thought but not known. But this runs into the problem of explaining the conceptual status of such a postulate. What content can 'thought' lay claim to, if it is placed wholly beyond the realm of experience? Either it has no content, in which case its religious usefulness is dubious, or it has some content, in which case it cannot be said that it is *sheer* mystery, altogether beyond the reach of our concepts. In particular, it is self-contradictory to say that 'we cannot apply to the noumenal Real any of the distinctions with which we structure our phenomenal, including our religious, experience', because this presupposes that we know something about the Real in order to be able to assert this.

(2) Hick indeed gives the Real a great deal of content, because he seems to want to ascribe causal properties to it in its role of

transforming religious subjects from 'self-centredness to reality-centredness'. But no theory of causality is offered, which would help to explain how it performs this role. Hick's response when faced with the possibility of a Marxist saint is to say that the saintliness must be caused by the Real, even though he does not realize it. But, if this assertion is not to lapse into a tautology, we must have some independent characterization of the Real, other than its said transformative powers, together with an account of its purported causation. Hick claims to be offering a hypothesis; but it is not clear how this hypothesis can effectively be tested.

(3) Indeed, the very notion of 'the transformation of human existence from self-centredness to Reality-centredness' as a criterion of an 'authentic manifestation of the Real' is question-begging. What counts towards such transformation will itself vary from religion to religion and there is no Archimedean human position that can mediate between religions as a whole. A position that did attempt such mediation would merely be another position, one among many. Hick's own position is much influenced by theistic speculation in a way that belies its purportedly neutral intent; I cannot, for example, imagine a Theravada Buddhist being altogether happy with his description of the Real.

(4) The epistemological problem of adjudicating between different truth-claims is distinct from, though related to, the metaphysical question of the Real and its appearances, which is Hick's concern here. From the premises of (a) different conceptions of the Real in the world faiths and (b) a common transformation taking place in each of them, Hick concludes that this transformation must have a unitary cause. Quite aside from the absence of a causal account, there is the assumption that the different faiths are attempting to conceive of one and the same entity. But simply from the transformative effects, one has no reason for assuming a unitary ground, rather than equivalent or similar grounds. Each religion on this alternative model would make a distinction between 'reality' and 'appearance', but it would be an internal distinction made on internal criteria. There would be no way of postulating *the* Real, because this would imply a commensurability, the possibility of which Hick has not demonstrated.

26

Response

John Hick

I am grateful for these critical queries and disagreements. Much that I have tried to say here was said very briefly and has given rise to legitimate questions and suggested significant counter-considerations. Most of these can I think be met by further explanation, though some reflect deep differences of viewpoint which can be clarified but probably not resolved.

John Roth's contention is that 'in his speaking about "the Real *an sich*" Hick is doing the very thing that his own epistemology rules out'. For if the Real is so utterly transcendent that we know nothing about it, we can say nothing about it and should remain silent. This is certainly true; but not, as I shall try to show, on target. The suggestion under consideration is that we should postulate the Real as the noumenal ground of the different forms of religious experience-and-thought insofar as they are not simply human projections. I have not offered a positive argument in my exposition (though I have elsewhere) for the belief that religious experience is not purely delusory but is in part a cognitive response to a reality beyond us; but it is from this starting point, of an acceptance of the basically veridical character of religious experience, that I want to interpret the history of religions. Such an interpretation, making sense both of the phenomenological variety of the different traditions and of their character as responses to the transcendent, requires us to postulate the Real as their ultimate ground. We cannot describe this ground in the terms used to describe its phenomenal manifestations, for it is not another such manifestation. We can, however, refer to it as the noumenal reality which is thought-and-experienced in these different ways. There is, surely, no contradiction in postulating a reality beyond the experienceable realm to account for what we find in that realm.

Stephen Davis takes up the same point. He asks how it is that, if the Real is beyond the scope of human thought and experience, one can apply to it such concepts as 'ground', 'beyond', 'real', 'explain' and 'one'. But the postulated Real is not beyond the scope of concepts as such. This would entail that that to which we are referring cannot be referred to! Accordingly, purely formal statements, which do not tell us concretely what the Real is like, can nevertheless be made about it. A trivial example is the statement that the Real has the attribute of being referred to. An important example is that the Real is the ultimate transcendent reality which is experienced as the Gods and Absolutes of the religious traditions. To say this is to say something about the relation of the postulated Real to the phenomenal or experienceable realm, but not about its noumenal or unexperienceable nature.

Joseph Prabhu also has concerns in the same general area. He says that 'it is self-contradictory to say that "we cannot apply to the noumenal Real any of the distinctions with which we structure our phenomenal, including our religious, experience", because this presupposes that we know something about the Real, in order to be able to assert this'. Strictly speaking we do not *know* anything (in the strong sense of 'know') about the Real, but we can nevertheless postulate it in order to make sense from a religious point of view of the plurality of forms of religious experience-and-thought. It seems to me clear that no self-contradiction is involved in this move.

In the same general area of language about the Real, Christopher Ives, recognizing the parallel between the notions of the Real and of *śūnyatā*, distinguishes them by saying that whereas the Real is a 'thing', *śūnyatā* is not. This, I think, is an overstatement. When I refer to the Real as 'something' I merely mean that we can refer to it. I do not mean that it is a *thing* in the sense of an object, or substance, or entity, or being. As I put it in my essay, 'We cannot say that it is personal or impersonal, one or many, active or passive, substance or process, good or evil, just or unjust, purposive or purposeless'. The notion of the Real is very close to one understanding of *śūnyatā*, namely as the unknowable, unconceptualizable ground of everything. But whereas Zen generally identifies this with the world itself, directly experienced without ego-distortion, the hypothesis in my essay sees Zen *satori* as *one* authentic manifestation of the Real and allows for the possibility of other different but perhaps equally authentic manifestations. In Zen, the Real is experienced as totally immanent in and coterminous with the world; in the advaitic experience, as totally transcendent; and in most theistic experience, as both. The hypothesis offered in my exposition, as a global rather than a tribal theory (in this case that of the Mahayana Buddhist tribe), seeks to take account of all these different ways of experiencing the Real.

In a related area, Davis asks for the evidence for such a theory. The only meaning that 'evidence' can have in this context is as referring to the range of facts which the theory renders intelligible. This comprises the religious experience of humanity through the ages. But the theory is not that the Jahweh of Hebrew religious experience and the Emptiness (*śūnyatā*) of Zen experience are phenomenologically identical, or even similar, but on the contrary that they constitute very different experiences of the same ultimate reality. According to the theory, each arises at the interface between the transcendent Real and a human religious mentality, and is a joint product of human projection and transcendent presence. Thus, in supposing that the phenomenological dissimilarity of the experiences renders it absurd to regard them as different responses to the same noumenal reality, Davis has, I think, mistaken the nature of the theory under consideration.

Concerning the behavioural effects in human life of awareness of the Real, I do not agree with Prabhu that the profile of the trans- formed saint differs essentially from tradition to tradition. In each case the authentic saint is one who has turned from self to the Real as apprehended within his or her tradition. The spiritual quality of an unself-centred transparency to a universal reality which links the saints to their fellows in agape/karuna is discernably the same. The basic similarity of this transformation of human existence from self- centredness to Reality-centredness, in spite of the fact that that Reality is conceived and perceived in the different ways found within the great world faiths, constitutes a major reason for pre- suming that within each tradition men and women are responding to the same ultimate reality.

There is thus an answer to Davis's and Prabhu's question, why postulate only *one* such Reality? Because the unity of the Real (strictly, not numerical unity but 'The One without a second') is the simplest hypothesis with which to account for the data, particularly the common human transformation. It would be gratuitous to suppose two or more Reals, none of which would then be truly ultimate. And why – Davis further asks – suppose that the good aspects of religion in history stem from its being partly a response to the Real, and the evil aspects from its being partly a creation of human nature? Because this is what the religious traditions severally

hold; and our hypothesis offers a religious interpretation of them
collectively.

   Returning to Roth, the distinction between the ultimate Real and
its manifestations to human consciousness does not lead, as he
supposes, to the conclusion that 'all the great religions say essentially
the same thing'. On the contrary, it starts from the fact that they
each say something different, the discourse of one being centred on
the Holy Trinity, of another on Brahman, of another on Allah, of
another on the Dharmakaya, of another on Jahweh, and so on. But
in order to acknowledge the authenticity of each, as cognitive
response as well as, in part, delusory projection, I have suggested
that we need to see them as constituting different ways of conceiving, experiencing and responding to the Real from within our
different ways of being human. This may or may not be an illuminating suggestion, but it is certainly not accurately characterized as
the idea that the religions all say the same thing. One aim of the
hypothesis is precisely to make sense of the phenomenological
differences of the different traditions other than by saying that one is
true and the rest false. It is, however, the case (and here I simply
disagree with Roth) that from the point of view of the phenomenology of religion each of the great traditions exhibits a soteriological
structure, including the vision of some kind of limitlessly better state
which is possible for all human beings.

   Roth's positive suggestion that we should seek to detach religious
from political differences, so that the people of the different traditions can disagree without trying to kill one another, seems to be
entirely appropriate and constructive; but it should not be seen as an
alternative to the search for an intellectual understanding which
acknowledges both their individual authenticity and their individual uniqueness.

   The hypothesis offered in my essay, in the search for such an
understanding, is simply an affirmation of the basic religious conviction of the reality of the transcendent or ultimate, but stated in
terms of the plurality of major religious traditions instead of – as has
been more usual – only one. The hypothesis thus belongs to the
emerging subject of global as distinguished from tribal theology.

   John Cobb's contention, however, is that such a theory must
conflict with an important element in the positive teaching of each of
the great traditions. And in so far as each has claimed that its own
experience and understanding of the Real, or the Ultimate, is the
only fully authentic one, a pluralistic theory does indeed question

this aspect of their self-understanding. For it is a meta-theory, standing back from the different traditions and suggesting how they may each constitute an authentic response, both cognitive and practical, to the Ultimate Reality to which the others are also responding through different sets of concepts, images, mythologies and spiritual practices. Because the traditions are human and culturally conditioned, none constitutes a perfect response – though each has committed the natural human error of assuming its own unique superiority.

It may or may not prove possible for the traditions gradually to de-emphasize and eventually leave behind their claim to be the only 'true religion'. If we think along the rigid lines laid out in Davis's last paragraph we shall not be able to achieve a global religious outlook. But we do not have to restrict ourselves in this way. For there is within each tradition a recognition that the focus of its worship or contemplation is, in its ultimate nature, beyond human character-ization. To take the two instances to which Cobb refers, the Kena Upanishad says of Brahman, 'There the eye goes not, speech goes not, nor the mind' (1.3), and the Qu'ran says that Allah is 'beyond what they describe' (6:101). (Likewise St Thomas says that 'The First Cause surpasses human understanding and speech' [*In !ibrum de causis*, 6].) Thus these traditions each have their own internal basis for the thought that that which they know in their own terms may be known by others in other terms. To affirm the Real is thus not to deny *nirguna* Brahman and *al Haq*: rather, these are the Hindu and Muslim ways of referring to the ultimate transcendent Reality. Indeed at some point within each tradition we find the thought that the Real may be known in many ways. Thus the Vedas say 'The real is one but sages name it variously'; and the Muslim mystic Rumi said of the different religions, 'The lamps are many but the Light is one'.

It is, of course, possible to see this pluralistic view as rejecting the deepest intuitions of each tradition. This is indeed how it has generally been seen in the past. But it is also possible to see it as pointing to the larger vision implicit within each tradition, to which each is capable of rising as it transcends its entrenched claim to unique normativeness. In recommending this wider vision it needs to be stressed again and again that to suppose that Brahman and Allah (and the other personae and impersonae) are different mani-festations of the Real, rather than being the unmanifest Real *an sich*, is not to suppose that each of them is unreal, or false. It is to suppose that there is a plurality of valid ways of thinking, experiencing and responding to the Real. In my opinion, this is the way forward for religious thinking today.

Index